MYSTERIES OF THE UNIVERSE

Attention Authors

'We Convert Fighters into Writers'. That's the motto of Manas Publications since more than four decades. Our message to the world is that India can win the battle not only by the bullet but also by the pen. There is no dearth of intellectuals in our country, but their knowledge is confined to them only. No sincere effort has been made by any other publisher to channelise their knowledge in national interest. That is why the talent of a large number of intellectuals remains latent. An author transforms his knowledge into a manuscript, and it is our job to spread his/her knowledge by converting it into a beautiful book. For over four decades, Manas has been motivating the intellectuals by publishing their manuscripts and would like to publish your manuscript too. If you or your colleagues have any manuscript ready for publication or are working on it, kindly contact us with detailed synopsis and list of contents. We will transform your work into a valuable publication. If you wish, we can also suggest you the suitable subjects for writing the books related to your area of expertise. Manas is known for its publishing quality and commitments. We take utmost care in production and give wide publicity to the book as well as its author through our national and international distribution network.

MYSTERIES OF THE UNIVERSE

Shashi Ranjan Kumar, IAS
(Government of India)

Manas Publications
(We Convert Fighters into Writers)
New Delhi - 110 002 (INDIA)

MANAS PUBLICATIONS
(We Convert Fighters into Writers)
(Publishers, Library Suppliers, Importers & Exporters)
4402/5-A, Ansari Road (Opp. HDFC Bank)
Darya Ganj, New Delhi - 110 002 (India)
Phones: Off.: 011-23260783, 23265523, Res.: 011-23842660
E-mail: manaspublications@gmail.com
manaspublications@yahoo.com
Website: www.manaspublications.in

ISBN 978-81-7049-553-6
₹ 595

Designed by
Veronica Grafic Arts

Printed in India at
R.K. Print Services, Delhi

Published by Mrs Suman Lata for
Manas Publications
4402/5-A, Ansari Road (Opp HDFC Bank),
Darya Ganj, New Delhi - 110002 (INDIA)

To

My Friend, Companion, Love

and

Wife

KALPANA

Contents

Acknowledgements

This book has been written over a long period of five to six years in fits and starts whenever I got a little respite after finishing the regular work, and the fact that I could devote this time solely for writing only confirms the indulgence with which my wife treated me during that period. Therefore, first I must thank her for not only being generous but also for being my first reader, who apart from improving my English, took pains to point out whether my narratives were simple enough to be appealing.

Although this book has been written in the last five to six years, its foundation has been laid much earlier, and during which I have learnt and benefited a great deal from a large number of friends, colleagues and acquaintances. Thanks are therefore due to them as well.

Finally, I must reserve my sincerest thanks for Anant, my friend since I entered the hallowed portals of IIT Delhi in 1985, for meticulously going through the entire manuscript, with microscopic eyes, noticing smallest of errors, suggesting structural changes in the book and helping improve the text wherever he found it was lacking in clarity.

Shashi Ranjan Kumar

Introduction

The first brush with science is always exhilarating, like when I learnt the concept of infinity in mathematics or that the earth is round, and not flat. All objects around us are countable, finite in size, so it is difficult to comprehend infinity - something that has no end. Imagine a very large number, in fact the largest that your mind can conceive, add one to it and you find a number greater than the greatest you just thought of. You can repeat the process, keep on counting, fill all the pages, and yet you never reach the end. This left me bewildered. And then I learnt that it is the earth that goes round the Sun, and not otherwise, and that there are other planets in the solar system, which move around the Sun in huge circles. Further, to my amazement, I came to know that the Sun is just one of billions of stars in the Milky Way galaxy, and so on.

Science enables us to understand the physical phenomena of the world, but more importantly, it contests dogmas, howsoever strongly held they may be, and encourages us to ask fundamental questions, the answers to which may not always be available. At a deeper level, science is a pursuit of truth, and so is philosophy. Remember, that science as a discipline is not very old, and before that the study of natural phenomena was within the purview of 'natural philosophy', a term which was in vogue even during the nineteenth century. It was, therefore, only fitting that the greatest work of science was named *Mathematical Principles of Natural Philosophy* by Sir Isaac Newton. Science is based on quantitative reasoning and experimentation as opposed to philosophy, which relies on qualitative reasoning. Science does not claim that it has found the truth, but it has certainly devised a method of finding truth. Like philosophy, it also makes assumptions, but conclusions derived from them are verifiable by empirical evidence.

Science has made tremendous progress since Copernicus turned astronomy on its head by breaking the consensus that the earth was at the centre of the universe, which had existed for more than a millennium. It has contributed so much in the progress of humankind that the material civilisation of today would be unrecognisable without it. Yet, I think it was not driven by the impulse of material advancement, but by our curiosity to find the truth, which indeed is the most beautiful pursuit in the world. Therefore, what I am really interested in is how much science, as also philosophy, has been able to answer the eternal questions staring at mankind.

My own curiosity in these questions was triggered by different events in life, at least some of which I have vivid recollections. I recall our family being visited by an astrologer when I was young. He was an expert in reading horoscopes. He predicted our life span down to the minutes and seconds by resorting to some complex calculations of planetary movements. I was amazed at the confidence with which he spoke, and at that moment a thought crossed my mind: If I knew exactly when I was going to die, wouldn't I take steps to prevent it? The fear of death also left me longing for something that would make me immortal. On another occasion – this was in an M Tech class – the professor was teaching the processing and transmission of digital signals, which are transmitted as streams of 0s and 1s. But some of 0s become 1s and some 1s turn into 0s when they are received due to noise inherent in the medium. If there is no noise in the medium, ie the error rate is zero, the signals are received without any distortion. Curiously, if the error rate is 100%, all the 0s become 1s and all 1s, 0s. The original signal can be recovered at the receiving end by simply converting 0s into 1s and 1s into 0s. Ergo, a perfect communication channel is as good as a completely imperfect channel, the cyclic nature of things.

This book consists of six chapters, each dealing with one set of questions, which are as relevant today as they were any time before. And in this, the most significant is: How the universe came into existence? An item, as small as a needle, requires raw materials, machines and human expertise for production. How was this giant universe, that runs billions of light years across, created? Who created it? What forces hold it together? And so on. In Chapter 1 "When It All Began" we will try and understand how science has grappled with these questions since the dawn of humanity. It presents a history of astronomy since the days of Aristotle and Ptolemy, when the earth was considered to be at the centre of the universe. Now, of course, we know that we are nowhere near the centre and the universe itself is expanding at an accelerating rate.

The second most significant question before us is the emergence of life on earth, which is buzzing all around us. Its sheer variety is amazing – from the simplest one-celled bacteria to the most complex, human beings. In the beginning, there was a consensus that all creatures were created by God – this is called creationism, and many people still believe in it. But this view has almost become untenable due to efforts made by scientists over centuries. And yet we are far from fully unravelling the mystery called life.

Life is indeed beautiful but it is also ephemeral; sooner or later it must come to an end. There is only one thing certain after being born, and that is death. Between life and death, there is only a tenuous thread of consciousness. We are not only aware of death but also of how much of life has gone by and how much is left, because we have been endowed with the faculty to perceive and measure the passage of time, in a way that no other species can. Death can be scary, a journey into a territory that is completely unknown. And that is why the desire to understand and conquer it has persisted despite any apparent success. Life, death and immortality are the subject matter of Chapter 2 titled "Is the Search for Immortality Futile".

What do you want in life? If this simple question is asked to different people, you will get different answers. Some want money, some power and some fame. But if you ask why you want money, or fame, or power, and persist with this line of enquiry, in the end you are likely to get a pretty common answer: Happiness. Everybody is ultimately in search of one thing and one alone, and that is happiness. But how do we attain happiness? There is a line of thought which advocates that acquisition is the key to happiness. The grandiose material civilisation that we have built is testimony to this. It emphasises on more: More consumption per capita of steel, electricity, cement, more mobile phones, more computers and so on. The material culture first creates a feeling of deprivation and then it tempts, solicits and, after having entangled you in desire, offers satisfaction. We enjoy the fruits of materialism but we also know that the enjoyment is temporary and as soon as it is over, the desire for more resurfaces.

However, there is an exactly opposite way of being happy. It relies on less. The less the craving, the less is the need. In one, you move outward in the spiral of desire towards infinity, in the other, inward towards *shunya,* that is zero, a state of desirelessness. *Isavasya Upanishad* says: *Tena tyakten bhunjitha.* How do you enjoy? You enjoy by renouncing. If there is no desire, there cannot be any misery. If you desire nothing, you have everything. You are the richest because no desire has been left unfulfilled. Equally, if all the desires are fulfilled, there cannot be any misery. Both the arguments are valid but both the states are difficult to achieve. Chapter 3 "Will We Ever Be Happy" is a multidisciplinary exploration of understanding of happiness and ways of attaining it. The chapter begins with ancient Hindu-Buddhist thoughts on happiness, and then delves into the attempt to measure both objective and subjective well-being by economists and psychologists.

Beauty, it is said, lies in the eyes of beholder, but where does reality lie? Does it also lie only in the perception of the observer or it exists independent of it? A glass and a plate are kept on a table, but each is unaware of the existence of the other, and reality does not manifest unless a conscious observer is present. This appears counter intuitive and an absurd proposition: Does the glass on the table not exist when I am not there? Even if I leave the table and go elsewhere, the glass continues to exist. Moreover, whoever observes this glass finds it exactly the same as I find it - of the same shape, size and colour. If everybody agrees with this description of the glass, it is perfectly legitimate to conclude that the glass is an independent physical reality, without the need of any observer. In Chapter 4 "How Real is Reality?" we will see that this is not so simple, and matter itself exists as a probability wave, which collapses and takes a position when it encounters the consciousness of the observer. The observer, therefore, becomes essential for 'the observed' to take a definite form. Further, unlike matter and energy, which are two constituents of physical reality, consciousness has defied any explanation or understanding. We know what matter and energy are made up of, we have found mathematical equations that govern them and we are able to quantify and measure them, but consciousness continues to elude us. It is a non-physical reality that we do not comprehend.

We are almost hardwired to think about the future - and this ranges from soothsaying to predicting the behaviour of the stock market. Even animals do a bit of planning while catching their prey. A tiger must be assessing its distance from the prey, the speed with and direction in which it may flee and the required speed to catch it. However, future can be foretold only if the events are predetermined. And this implies that the universe is completely deterministic, leaving no space for free will to operate. But we do have free will to influence the course of events. If you throw a ball to me, I have the option either to catch or leave it. More importantly, the material world itself is not fully deterministic as we shall see in Chapter 5, "Is Future Predictable?", which explores the age old dichotomy between free will and determinism and seeks an answer to the question, or whether, in fact, it is possible to predict the future. The chapter covers the discovery of four fundamental forces in nature, how the idea of scientific determinism that took roots in the early 19th century was shaken by the discovery of wave-particle duality.

In the final Chapter 6 "On the Razor's Edge: Why Balance is Essential in Life" we shall trace the history of the universe since the big bang, the formation of our galaxy, the birth of the solar system and the earth, the emergence of the simplest form of life and the gradual evolution of complex species like us. In this journey, we shall look at the evidence of fine tuning in life and try to answer the question: Why is balance essential in life? Buddha preached that extremes should be avoided. If the string of a *Veena* is tightened excessively, it will break; on the other hand if it is left slack, it will not produce beautiful music. Thus, Buddha explained the significance of balance and harmony in life, the middle path.

In the end, a few words on the format that has been followed in the chapters would be in order. They are written in a chronological order so that scientific developments can be appreciated in the right historical perspective. I have also included philosophical viewpoint, particularly the Hindu-Buddhist outlook, on the subjects, to provide the readers a complete picture of human effort in discovering the truth. Many epochal experiments have been described in the book, and in presenting them I have tried to strike a fine balance between the need to provide sufficient details and to avoid unnecessary complexity. It has been my endeavour throughout the book to express complex ideas in simple language so that any person with very little or even no background in science can substantially, if not fully, appreciate them. How much I have succeeded in this, only the readers can judge, but I will have little hesitation in accepting the failure should they hold an opinion contrary to this.

1

When It All Began?

> The cosmos springs into view simultaneously with the seer and that there is no detailed process of creation ... It is quite similar to the creations in dream where the experiencer springs up simultaneously with the objects of experience. – *Ramana Maharshi*

> God is always invented to explain those things that you do not understand. Now, when you finally discover how something works ... you don't need him anymore. But ... you leave him to create the universe because we haven't figured that out yet. – *Richard P Feynman*

Of all the questions that have been conceived by human intellect, those about the origin and nature of the universe have been the most daunting: Who created the universe? How and when did it come to exist? What existed before its existence? Will the universe come to an end or is it unborn and eternal? These questions are as old as human existence. The Sun straddling across majestically during the day and countless twinkling stars, planets and the waxing and waning of the moon in the night sky must have fascinated our forefathers – we can recall our own childhood memories of staring at the sky with bewilderment, not knowing anything about the deepest mysteries it hid. Equally, natural phenomena caused tremendous anxiety to them. No wonder ascribing them to divine intervention was prevalent in many civilizations. The vastness of space intimidated mankind, making its existence seem insignificant, but humans are endowed with the faculty of observation and analysis, using which we attempt to understand the universe and our place in it.

Earth is Round, and Not Flat

In ancient times, the Earth was believed to be a flat disc – a self-evident truth that did not require any proof – until Aristotle, who for the first time argued that the earth was spherical in shape. He knew that lunar eclipses occurred when the earth blocked the sunlight from reaching the moon. Therefore, if the Earth was flat, the shape of its shadow on the moon would be a straight line and not a curve:

> If the earth were not spherical, eclipses of the moon would not exhibit segments of the shape which they do. As it is, in its monthly phases the moon takes on all varieties of shape – straight-edged, gibbous, and concave – but in the eclipses the boundary is always convex. Thus, if the eclipses are due to the interposition of the earth, the shape must be caused by its circumference, and the earth must be spherical.[1]

He offered another reason in support of his proposition:

> Observation of the stars also shows not only that the earth is spherical but that it is of no great size, since a small change of position on our part southward or northward visibly alters the circle of the horizon, so that the stars above our heads change their position considerably, and we do not see the same stars as we move to the North or South. Certain stars are seen in Egypt and the neighbourhood of Cyprus, which are invisible in the more northerly lands, and stars which are continuously visible in the northern countries are observed to set in the others. This proves both that the earth is spherical and that its periphery is not large, for otherwise such a small

> change of position could not have had such an immediate effect. For this reason, those who imagine that the region around the Pillars of Heracles joins on to the regions of India, and that in this way the ocean is one, are not, it would seem, suggesting anything utterly incredible.[2]

Eratosthenes went one step further and actually estimated the circumference of the earth. He knew that on June 21st in the town of Syene in southern Egypt (today Aswan) the noontime sun was reflected in a deep well, meaning that it was right overhead and it did not cause any shadow. Eratosthenes himself lived in Alexandria - a city established by Alexander the Great - about 5,000 stadia north of Syene (the stadium, the size of a sports arena, was a unit of distance used by the Greeks). In Alexandria the sun on the corresponding date did not quite reach zenith, and vertical objects still threw a short shadow. Eratosthenes established that the direction of the noon sun differed from the zenith by an angle that was 1/50 of the circle, and from that he estimated the circumference of the earth to be 2,50,000 (50 × 5,000) stadia. Unfortunately, there is no unanimity amongst scientists today as to how much exactly is one stadium, and with estimates of one stadium varying from 157 metre to 209 metre, Eratosthenes calculation had a variation of 2 to 30% (39,250–52,250 km) from the modern value of the Earth's circumference of 40,075 km. However, this was a great leap forward despite its approximation because of the underlying simplicity and elegance of the idea.

Everything Revolves Around the Earth

Aristotle also presented a rudimentary model of the universe that consisted of eight transparent concentric spheres nestled into one another with the Earth lying at the centre. The eight spheres contained five known planets at that time - Venus, Mercury, Mars, Jupiter and Saturn - and the Sun, the Moon and the fixed stars. The spheres revolved around the Earth in uniform circular motion causing days and nights and other celestial phenomena. Since everything fell towards the Earth, Aristotle thought the earth lay at the centre of the universe. However, Aristotelian model of fixed Earth did not go unchallenged as Aristarchus of Samos, who was born only 12 years after the death of Aristotle, presented an alternative sun-centric hypothesis. The historical records are not sufficient to conclude whether his idea received widespread support. In fact, the original work of Aristarchus did not survive and the earliest mention of his work is found in Archimedes' *The Sand Reckoner*.

Aristotelian idea was refined into a complete cosmological model by another Greek, Claudius Ptolemy, who lived in Alexandria in the AD 2nd century, when the city had become a part of the Roman Empire. He wrote a mathematical and astronomical treatise, *Mathematike Syntaxis*, which was subsequently translated in Arabic, *al-majisti*, probably in the 9th century, and from Arabic to Latin, *Almagest* – the name which has struck since then. *Almagest* is the second most important scientific contribution of the ancient Greek civilisation after Euclid's *Elements*, which laid the foundation of geometry and number theory. It is from *Almagest*, the most authoritative ancient text on astronomy, that we get the details of Ptolemaic model.

Ancient Greeks, at the time of Ptolemy, were aware that the stars moved from east to west during the night, but their relative positions remained fixed. However, Mercury, Venus, Mars, Jupiter and Saturn changed their positions relative to fixed stars from night to night, and since they wandered in the sky, they earned the name wandering stars or planets. They appeared to move against the constellations of stars a little farther east when observed at a fixed time on successive nights. The Sun also appeared to drift eastward with respect to the stars, completing one full circle in a year. This was easily explained by Ptolemy by arguing that the

Earth was at the centre and Moon, Mercury, Venus, Sun, Mars, Jupiter and Saturn revolved around it – we now know that it accounted for the revolution of the planets around the Sun. The behaviour of Mars, however, was more perplexing as every two years or so, its eastward progress slowed down, stopped and then reversed from east to west. After a while, this westward journey also slowed down and stopped, and finally Mars resumed its eastward movement, almost forming a loop in the sky.

The apparent retrograde motion of Mars is caused by the difference in period of revolution of the Earth and Mars around the Sun – while the Earth completes one revolution around the Sun in 365 days, Mars does the same in 687 days. Therefore, the Earth overtakes Mars about every twenty-six months, like a faster athlete in an inner track going past his rival in the adjacent outer track. Although both planets move in an eastward direction, the earth moves faster making Mars to appear drifting westward during the period when it overtakes Mars.

How did Ptolemy's geocentric model explain the retrograde motion of planets? He first assumed that the planets moved along a smaller circle called epicycle and the centre of the epicycle revolved around the Earth in a larger circle known as the deferent. The entire system of deferent and epicycle itself rotate once every twenty-four hours – this mimicked the rotation of the earth on its axis. Ptolemy also considered the axial rotation of the earth but discarded the proposition arguing that no such motion was felt and if it indeed spun on its axis, a stone thrown upwards would land at a different spot. He further argued that the enormous centrifugal force due to the axial rotation of the earth (the speed of earth at the equator is approximately 1,650 km per hour) would tear it apart. Had he stuck to this idea, there would have been no need to rotate the entire system of deferent and epicycle once every twenty four hours in his model.

Let us take a thin metal ring of large radius and a thick ring of small radius. The small ring has two holes such that they lie exactly opposite to each other. Now the large ring is cut open at one point and the two ends are pierced through the two holes of the small ring and they are joined again so that it can freely slide on the circumference of the larger ring. Now imagine a bead that runs along the circumference of the small ring (epicycle) while the small ring itself slides on the large ring (deferent) with constant speed. The bead represents Mars, and the centre of the large ring, the earth. Mars completed one revolution along the epicycle in a year while the centre of its epicycle circled once around the earth in 1.88 years. In the Ptolemaic model, both motions took place from west to east, therefore, Mars appeared to move from west to east (normal motion) to an observer on the earth during the period it was travelling along the portion of the epicycle outside the deferent, but on the portion of the epicycle lying within the deferent, it moved from east to west (retrograde motion).

But the complexity did not end here: In some region of the sky, Mars was observed to move faster during the retrograde motion, executing a smaller loop, and in another it formed a bigger loop moving slowly, which could not be accounted for by uniform circular motion on deferent and epicycle. Ptolemy, therefore, refined the model by shifting the earth a little off-centre of the deferent, making the orbits of the planets around the earth, eccentric. When the planets were closer to the earth they moved faster and vice versa. Further, he imagined a point called equant on the opposite side of the earth such that the centre of the deferent lay between the earth and the equant. The planets revolved with uniform angular speed – sweeping equal angle in equal time – with respect to the equant and not the centre of the deferent. Ptolemy succeeded in explaining the observed motion of the planets by these two adjustments in the model and although they were minor, Aristotelian principles that the earth was at the centre of the universe and the planets revolved around it in perfect circles were certainly compromised.

Ptolemy died around the middle of the AD second century, and for a long time thereafter, there was hardly any advancement in astronomy. Almost three centuries later, in the year AD 476, Aryabhata, an Indian mathematician and astronomer, was born in Pataliputra (modern Patna), who used the same method as that of Eratosthenes to measure the circumference of the Earth. It is now almost certain that he conducted the experiment at the astronomical site of Ujjain, which still survives. Ujjain in central India, like Syene in Egypt, lies on the tropic of cancer. He measured the circumference of earth to be 4967 yojanas (the measuring unit of distance in the ancient India which is equal to 5 miles). He therefore significantly improved the computation of the Earth's circumference to 39,968.0582 km, which is only 0.2% smaller than the actual value of 40,075.0167 km. Eratosthenes's calculation is less accurate because Syene and Alexandria do not lie on the same longitude and the exact value of stadia is not known. Aryabhata was also able to calculate the diameter of the earth since he knew the value of π (3.1416) accurate to five significant figures:

> Add four to 100, multiply by eight, and then add 62,000. The result is approximately the circumference of a circle of which the diameter is 20,000.[3]

"As a man in a boat going forward sees a stationary object moving backward just so at Lanka a man sees the stationary asterisms [groups of stars] moving backward (westward) in a straight line."[4] Aryabhata not only clearly recognised the axial rotation of the earth but also provided the angular velocity of its rotation: one minute (one sixtieth of a degree) in one *prana* (4 seconds), which means 15 degree/hour or 360 degree in 24 hours. Yet the idea of the planets circling the earth did not occur to Aryabhata, and unfortunately later Indian astronomers not only rejected his concept of relative motion but also "tried to manoeuvre his text so as to obtain just the contrary meaning."[5]

Indian and Arab astronomers predicted planetary positions with greater accuracy by making small adjustments here and there, but without making any fundamental change in the geocentric model. However, in the early part of 16th century, Nilkantha Somasutvan of Kerala School of Astronomy deviated from the traditional geocentric model. He proposed that the five planets orbited the sun in eccentric circles, which, in turn, revolved around the earth. "It is well known that the Indian astronomers were mainly interested in the successful computations of the longitudes and latitudes of the sun, [the] moon and the planets and were not much worried about proposing models of the universe."[6] Perhaps it was this fundamental weakness that prevented them from developing a full-fledged heliocentric theory, which was being worked upon by Nilkantha's contemporary, Nicolaus Copernicus, a priest, in faraway Poland.

Sun is at the Centre of the Universe

Nicolaus Copernicus challenged Aristotelian-Ptolemaic stationary earth hypothesis by arguing that if the planets and the fixed stars revolved around the earth daily, they would be travelling at a very high speed in order to cover huge distances in twenty four hours, and consequently they would experience centrifugal forces of much greater magnitude than a spinning earth ever would. He, therefore, rejected Ptolemy's claim that the earth would burst asunder due to outward pull of rotation. Copernicus further asserted that everything attached to the earth, including the atmosphere, also rotated with it once in twenty four hours and that was why clouds did not appear to move in the opposite direction at high speed and a stone thrown upward from the earth did not lose its eastward motion and fell exactly at the same spot from where it was thrown. The earth, in addition to its axial rotation, also revolved around the sun, and so did other planets, thus firmly putting the sun at the centre of the universe:

> At rest, however, in the middle of everything is the sun. For in this most beautiful temple, who would place this lamp in another or better position than that from which it can light up the whole thing at the same time? For, the sun is not inappropriately called by some people the lantern of the universe, its mind by others, and its ruler by still others. [Hermes] the Thrice Greatest labels it a visible god, and Sophocles' *Electra*, the all-seeing. Thus indeed, as though seated on a royal throne, the sun governs the family of planets revolving around it.[7]

Although Copernicus had conceived the Sun-centric planetary model almost thirty years ago, he was reluctant to share his ideas fearing public ridicule, and he finally published his book *De revolutionibus orbium coelestium* (*On the Revolutions of the Celestial Spheres*) in 1543, just before his death, and that too only after relentless persuasion from his friends. He was rather candid about his procrastination:

> Those who know that the consensus of many centuries has sanctioned the conception that the earth remains at rest in the middle of the heaven as its centre would, I reflected, regard it as an insane pronouncement if I made the opposite assertion that the earth moves. Therefore I debated with myself for a long time whether to publish the volume which I wrote to prove the earth's motion...[8]

While Copernicus abandoned the long held dogma of stationary earth, he continued with another, that is, the circle being the perfect shape for the movement of heavenly bodies; not surprisingly, therefore, his planets revolved around the sun in circles. But this posed a problem to his model because the planets were not observed to move at uniform speed around the sun – they speeded up and slowed down. Therefore, he borrowed Ptolemy's epicycles to explain the non-uniform motion of the planets, and used two epicycles instead of one, complicating the rather simple and elegant model of the planetary system. Let us recount the complete model presented by Copernicus: the earth rotated on its axis once daily and the planets revolved around the sun in circular orbits (with epicycles). The axis of rotation of earth was not perpendicular to the orbital plane of the earth but was tilted by 23.5°. The fixed stars were immovable and the moon revolved around the earth in 28 days. The tilted axis of rotation better explained the variation of seasons on the earth and the heliocentric model elegantly accounted for the retrograde motion of the planets.

De revolutionibus is today recognised as one of the most revolutionary scientific treatise of all times, but it remained on the margin of acceptance for quite a long time after publication and contrary to the popular narrative, it encountered more scientific scrutiny than religious opposition. Though its central idea violated the Christian doctrine of immovable earth, there was hardly any reaction from the Church, and the book was placed on *Index Librorum Prohibitorum* (Index of Prohibited Books) in 1616 – 73 years after its publication – only when it started gaining recognition. The heliocentric model could not get immediate acclaim because Copernicus failed to detect any stellar parallax, the ultimate proof of the revolution of the earth around the sun, to which we shall now turn.

Imagine you are moving in a car on a highway from point A to B. When you look outside the window and fix your gaze on a near point C, it is found in line with a distant point D. But as you move towards B, C gradually moves backward and is found in line with another distant point E – this phenomenon is known as parallax. In Copernican model, the earth moves in a circular orbit around the sun, therefore, a person on the earth should observe a nearby star move against the background of distant stars when the earth travels from one point in the orbit to its diametrically opposite point, a distance of 300 million km. Copernicus knew that observing the annual stellar parallax would irrefutably confirm the heliocentric model, but unfortunately, he found no evidence of it, and therefore he was persuaded to believe that the stars were at incredibly large distances. (Proxima Centauri, the nearest star in our neighbourhood, shows parallax of less than 1 arc second, an angle which can be obtained by dividing a circle into more than 12,96,000 equal parts. Such a small angle could not have been observed with the naked eye - the telescope was not invented as yet.)

Tycho Falls Between Two Stools

Tycho Brahe was born three years after the death of Copernicus and was the last of the great astronomers - and perhaps the most prolific - who recorded the positions of celestial bodies with the naked eye. Tycho described the earth as "a lazy sluggish body unfit for motion" and wondered how Copernicus could ascribe any motion to such a body.[9] Tycho also turned the Copernicus's argument, that no stellar parallax was visible because the stars were too far away from the earth, against him. Since no parallax could be observed, it was apparent that it was less than the lowest Tycho could measure, and from this he estimated the minimum possible distance to a typical star. He also measured the angular diameter of the star and then arrived at the actual size of the star by simple multiplication, which turned out to be ridiculously large. (It was revealed later that the angular diameter of stars as measured by Tycho was highly exaggerated due to optical illusion - in reality the stars are much smaller than they appear to be):

> Then the stars of the third magnitude which are one minute in diameter will necessarily be equal to the entire annual orbit [of the earth], that is, they would comprise in their diameter 2,284 semi-diameters of the earth.... Deduce these things geometrically if you like, and you will see how many absurdities (not to mention others) accompany this assumption [of the motion of the earth] by inference.[10]

Tycho also found a simple method to test the veracity of Ptolemaic and Copernican hypotheses. The distance between the Earth and Mars in the Ptolemaic system was always larger than the distance between the earth and the sun – recall that Mars revolved around the earth in a larger circle than the sun. In Copernican system, however, the earth-Mars distance varied significantly. When the earth and Mars were on the opposite sides of the sun, the earth-Mars distance was greater than the earth-sun distance, and conversely, when the earth and Mars were on the same side of the sun, the distance between them was less than the earth-sun distance. Therefore, if the distance of Mars when it was closest to the earth could be measured, a simple comparison with the earth-sun distance would conclusively prove one of the two hypotheses.[11]

The distance to a celestial body from the earth was measured by diurnal parallax, that is, by observing the apparent angular displacement of the body against the backdrop of the distant stars between morning and evening. Since the diameter of the earth was known, the distance to the body could easily be obtained by simple geometry. Therefore, "Tycho's quest for the parallax of Mars was a driving factor during the golden years at his Uraniborg observatory in the 1580s. At first, when he found no parallax, he believed that the Copernican arrangement had to be rejected since Mars seemed, even at it closest approach, to be farther than the sun."[12] We now know that the diurnal parallax of Mars is at most 23 arc second, a value too little to be captured even by Tycho's sophisticated instruments. Further, he did not calculate solar parallax himself, but relied on highly exaggerated Ptolemaic value of 170 arc second, and therefore the conclusion he reached was inescapable.[13] Curiously, Tycho changed his opinion a few years later and interpreted his Mars observations differently, concluding that Mars indeed came closer to the earth than the sun. Yet he did not confirm the Copernican hypothesis and proposed a new mixed hypothesis, combining the features of Ptolemy and Copernicus.[14] Tycho's planets revolved around the sun, which, in turn, orbited the earth. It was essentially the same as Nilkantha's hypothesis presented half a century earlier.

As the curtain was drawing on the 16th century, the Ptolemaic model, which had reigned supreme for over a millennium, faced serious challenges from Copernicus and Tycho, though it was still widely accepted. If Tycho could better predict planetary positions, it was because he had gathered more accurate data at Uraniborg observatory, generously funded by the Danish king. The other two models could be suitably adjusted to give the same results. The motion of celestial bodies can be described with respect to any frame of reference because motion is relative. To a person standing on a railway platform, a passing train has a speed of say 60 km per hour. Equally, a person on the moving train observes the person standing on the platform move in the opposite direction, with the same speed. There is no preferred reference frame with respect to which motion can be described objectively. We can assume the earth to be at complete rest and depict the motion of all celestial bodies with respect to it. Similarly, any planet or the moon can also serve as a reference point equally well. If that is so, which one of these models represented the truth?

Copernicus began with perfect circular motion of celestial bodies, but had to borrow 'epicycles' from Ptolemy to match the observations with the predictions of his model. Tychonic system "might have been completed in detail by being furnished with excentrics and epicycles like its rival[s]"[15] but for the untimely death of Tycho. All the models also suffered from inconsistencies: Ptolemy had devised a complicated mechanism to explain the motion of the moon, which brought the moon at times twice as close to the earth, but the moon was never observed twice as big. Copernicus explained the retrograde motion of superior planets more elegantly but predicted stellar parallax, which was not seen and Tycho's universe had two centres, the earth and the sun, around which celestial bodies revolved. Neither on the basis of aesthetic appeal nor internal consistency could one model be preferred over the other. And it was in this utterly confused state that astronomy passed into the seventeenth century.

Tycho had gathered voluminous data on planetary positions but he lacked mathematical ability to analyse them. He was familiar with the work of Johannes Kepler, a German astronomer, who he invited for a meeting while he was in Prague for establishing a new observatory. He was hoping to employ the mathematical genius of Kepler to validate the Tychonic system. Kepler, on the other hand, had published his first major astronomical work, *Mysterium Cosmographicum* (The Cosmographic Mystery) in 1596, defending the Copernican system and needed Tycho's observations to empirically test and refine his theory. Kepler met Tycho in Febuary 1600 and agreed to become his assistant; their relationship was not only short-lived, as Tycho died in October 1601, but was also marred by acrimony and suspicion. Tycho was condescending and provided information to Kepler only in bits and pieces - perhaps he doubted his intention - which left Kepler resentful and frustrated. It was only after the unexpected demise of Tycho that Kepler gained complete access to his data.[16]

Kepler's mathematical analysis of rather accurate planetary observations recorded by Tycho revealed that the planets revolved not in circular but elliptical orbits with the sun at one of its foci. (An ellipse is an elongated circle; mathematically, the sum of distances from the two foci to any point on an ellipse is constant. A circle is a special type of ellipse whose both foci coincide.) He further stated that if a line was drawn from the sun to a planet, it would sweep equal area in equal time, meaning that the planets slowed down when they moved farther from the sun and vice versa. The refinement proposed by Kepler at once got rid of

Copernicus's epicycles, which were introduced to explain the apparent speeding up and slowing down of planets in their orbits, and the heliocentric model got a simpler and more elegant look. Although Kepler had discovered the laws of planetary motion by 1605, he published *Astronomia Nova* (New Astronomy) only in 1609 due to dispute with Tycho's family over legal rights to the data. In 1619, he also established a mathematical relationship between the orbital period and the mean distance of the planet from the sun, which is known as Kepler's third law of planetary motion.

Galileo Validates Copernicus, But Earns the Wrath of the Church

The following year, Galileo Galilei, an Italian polymath, was scanning the night sky of Padua with his newly built telescope when he discovered four objects in the vicinity of Jupiter. Initially he thought that they were stars, but they changed position relative to Jupiter on successive nights and shifted from one side of the planet to the opposite. This led him to conclude that they were the moons of Jupiter orbiting around it. Galileo's discovery established that there was nothing special about the earth that compelled celestial bodies to revolve around it. However, it was not the same as proving that they did not indeed revolve around the earth as claimed by the Ptolemaic model.

Galileo made another discovery in the very same year, but towards the end of it, which directly refuted the Ptolemaic model. He observed the phases of Venus - from crescent to gibbous to full, much like waxing and waning of the moon. In the Copernican model, the earth and Venus could be on the opposite side of the sun allowing the full face of Venus to be seen from the earth, and therefore Galileo's observation was entirely in agreement with its prediction. The sun, in the Ptolemaic model, revolved around the earth in a circular orbit completing one cycle in a year. Also, the planets moved along epicycles and the centres of the epicycles revolved around the earth. In case of inferior planets like Mercury and Venus, the centres of the epicycles were fixed to the orbit of the sun, meaning that they moved in tandem with the sun. Therefore, Venus always remained between the earth and the sun, preventing its full face from being seen from the earth.

Those who still believed in the inviolability of the stationary earth sought refuge in the Tychonic system, which explained the phases of Venus as successfully as Copernican system, but Galileo's observations inflicted a severe blow from which the Ptolemaic model could not recover. It is, therefore, not surprising that the growing evidence - as also support - for the Copernican system prompted the Church to prevent the spread of a belief it thought to be heretic. On 26th Febuary 1615, Galileo was summoned by Cardinal Robert Bellarmine at his palace in Rome and asked to abandon his belief in sun-centric system. Galileo was aware that Giordano Bruno, a fellow astronomer and philosopher, was ordered to be burnt at the stake in the year 1600 at the Inquisition presided over by the same Cardinal for arguing that stars were distant suns with their own planets, possibly containing life, and the universe was infinite with no celestial body as its centre. Galileo complied, and exactly a week later *De Revolutionibus* was placed on the Index of Prohibited Books by a decree of the Church:

> This Holy Congregation has also learned about the spreading and acceptance by many of the false Pythagorean doctrine, altogether contrary to the Holy Scripture, that the earth moves and the sun is motionless, which is also taught by Nicolaus Copernicus's *On the Revolutions of the Heavenly Spheres* and by Diego de Zuniga's *On Job*. This may be seen from a certain letter published by a certain Carmelite Father [Paolo Antonio Foscarini] ... in which the said Father tries to show that the above-mentioned doctrine of the sun's rest at the centre of the world and of the earth's motion is consonant with the truth

> and does not contradict Holy Scripture. Therefore, in order that this opinion may not advance any further to the prejudice of Catholic truth, the Congregation has decided that the books by Nicolaus Copernicus (*On the Revolutions of Spheres*) and by Diego de Zuniga (*On Job*) be suspended until corrected; but that the book of the Carmelite Father Paolo Antonio Foscarini be completely prohibited and condemned; and that all other books which teach the same be likewise prohibited, according to whether with the present decree it prohibits, condemns, and suspends them respectively.[17]

Galileo was silenced, but only temporarily; he was awaiting an opportune moment to lend support to the Copernican system. In 1623, Cardinal Maffeo Barberini, a friend and a fellow Florentine, was elected as the new Pope. He appeared to be more tolerant and believed that the Copernican system had little chance of getting validated and though astronomers might devise mathematical models to predict planetary positions, the real design of the cosmos would remain hidden from human scrutiny. Galileo started working on the *Dialogue Concerning the Two Chief World Systems* from 1624 and it was published eight years later after obtaining Church imprimatur. The book is written in the form of a conversation between three fictional characters: Salviati, a Copernican; Simplicio, a defender of the Ptolemaic world-view; and Sagredo, a neutral person who gradually comes to accept Salviati's arguments. The *Dialogue* caused such a furore that he was put on trial spread over three months in the year 1633. Kneeling down, with the *Bible* in his hand, he repudiated his belief in the Copernican system and was sentenced to imprisonment, which was later converted to house arrest. Galileo died in 1642 under arrest in his own house in Florence.

Newton Discovers the Universal Gravitation

The heliocentric model conceived by Copernicus, refined by Kepler and nearly confirmed by Galileo was awaiting a theory of physical cause that could explain the planetary motion instead of merely describing it. Kepler was the first to suggest that the sun provided the force that impelled the planets into motion and this force decreased as the distance from the sun increased, but he erroneously thought that the force between the sun and the planets was magnetic in nature. By the second half of the 17th century, consensus was emerging among scientists that the sun exerted a gravitational force on the planets. Robert Hooke believed that the magnitude of the gravitational force between the sun and the planets followed inverse square law, that is, the force of attraction quadrupled if the distance between them was halved. However, he did not provide any mathematical formulation of the force, nor could he derive Kepler's three laws of planetary motion from it. Later, Hooke alleged that Isaac Newton had not sufficiently acknowledged his contribution to the universal law of gravitation, which led to a bitter and long quarrel between them.

Isaac Newton was born in England in the year Galileo died, which of course was purely coincidental, but Newton was greatly indebted to Galileo - and indeed Copernicus, Tycho and Kepler. Until Galileo discovered the concept of inertia, it was thought that the state of rest was the natural state of every object - did an object set to motion not come slowly to rest? Galileo proposed something that was counter-intuitive at that time: a moving object came to rest because the surface on which it was moving exerted a frictional force on it, and therefore if there were no friction, the object would continue in its state of uniform linear motion. In other words, bodies have a natural tendency to resist any change in its state of motion. Newton borrowed the concept of inertia from Galileo and enunciated the first law of motion: an object will continue to be at rest or in uniform linear motion unless it is acted upon by an external force. The second law of motion provided the quantitative relation between the applied force and the change in motion:

"the alteration of motion is ever proportional to the motive force impressed; and is made in the direction of the right line in which that force is impressed."[18] However, the third law of motion - every action has an equal and opposite reaction - was indeed the original contribution of Newton.

Christiaan Huygens, a Dutch scientist, had figured out in 1659 that an object tied to a string was held in circular motion by the inward pull provided by the tension in the string. Therefore, it was not difficult to conclude that the planets would simply fly off tangentially if they were not pulled by the sun, but it was Newton who proposed that the force that kept the planets or moon in their orbits was the same that pulled any object towards the earth when thrown upwards. He performed a thought experiment in which he imagined a ball being thrown parallel to the earth's surface from some height. The ball would follow a curved path and hit the surface of the earth at some distance. What would happen if the initial speed of the imaginary ball was increased? It would travel a greater distance and hit the surface further away. He concluded that if the speed of the ball could be arbitrarily increased, the ball would not fall on the earth altogether but go round it:

> A projectile, if it was not for the force of gravity, would not deviate towards the earth, but would go off from it in a right line ... with a uniform motion if the resistance of the air was taken away. It is by its gravity that it is drawn aside perpetually from its rectilinear course, and made to deviate towards the earth, more or less, according to the force of its gravity, and the velocity of its motion. The less its gravity is, for the quantity of its matter, or the greater the velocity with which it is projected, the less will it deviate from a rectilinear course, and the farther it will go. If a leaden ball, projected from the top of a mountain by the force of gunpowder with a given velocity, and in a direction parallel to the horizon, is carried in a curve line to the distance of two miles before it falls to the ground; the same, if the resistance of the air were

> taken away, with a double or decuple velocity, would fly twice or ten times as far. And by increasing the velocity, we may at pleasure increase the distance to which it might be projected, and diminish the curvature of the line, which it might describe, till at last it should fall at the distance of 10, 30, or 90 degrees, or even might go quite round the whole earth....[19]

Newton extended the argument further by stating that any two bodies attracted each other with a force proportional to the quantities of matter contained in them and inversely proportional to the square of distance between them. This came to be known as the universal law of gravitation or the inverse square law, which mathematically yielded Kepler's laws of motion, putting a theoretical seal on the Copernican-Kepler model. Newton predicted the positions of planets more accurately and explained that the tides were caused by the gravitational force exerted by the moon and the sun. Newton published *Philosophiae Naturalis Principia Mathematica* (Mathematical Principles of Natural Philosophy) in 1687, arguably the most important scientific treatise ever written in the history of mankind, which contained the laws of motion and of universal gravitation.

What is the order of magnitude of gravitational force? The earth exerts a force of 9.8 Newton (Newton or N, in short, is a unit of force) on an object at its surface having mass of one kg. Although the solar mass is more than 3,00,000 times the earth's mass, the sun pulls the same object on the surface of the earth with a force of merely 0.006 N because of the large distance between the sun and the earth. If the distance between two objects is doubled, the force is reduced to one-fourth. The force diminishes but never becomes zero no matter how far the objects are away from each other; gravitation is a force which acts over infinite range.

In everyday life, force requires direct contact to exert and transmit itself, but gravitational force acts at a distance without any physical contact or a medium between two objects. Most scientists in the 17th century were not comfortable with action-at-a-distance force and clung to the idea that gravitation was some kind of a mechanical force. Newton abandoned this dogma and accepted the possibility of such a force, although he was unable to provide any explanation of how gravitational force acted over large distances. A letter that he wrote to theologian Richard Bentley in 1693, six years after the publication of the *Principia,* reflected his dilemma:

> It is inconceivable, that inanimate brute matter, should, without the mediation of something else, which is not material, operate upon and affect other matter without mutual contact.... [This] is to me so great an absurdity, that I believe no man, who has in philosophical matters a competent faculty of thinking, can ever fall into it. Gravity must be caused by an agent acting constantly according to certain laws; but whether this agent be material or immaterial, I have left to the consideration of my readers.[20]

The discovery of gravitational force ignited a debate on the size of the universe. It can be recalled that Ptolemy's universe consisted of concentric spheres with the earth at the centre and the outermost sphere containing the fixed stars. Copernicus had no doubt that "of all things visible, the highest is the heaven of the fixed stars" and he also reasoned that "the size of the universe is so great that the distance earth-sun is imperceptible in relation to the sphere of the fixed stars."[21] Even though Copernicus referred to the immense distance at which the sphere of stars lay, to infer from it, as some forcefully do, that he conceived of an infinite universe is stretching the argument too thin. It was Giordano Bruno, an Italian polymath, who made the daring attempt not only to propose an infinite universe but also to claim that stars had their own planetary systems, possibly containing life just like the earth.

If the universe was finite in size, it ran into serious problem with the law of universal gravitation. The stars on the edge of the universe would experience a net inward gravitational pull as there would be nothing to exert a balancing outward pull on them. These stars would not remain in a state of equilibrium and acquire an inward motion due to gravitational pull. As a result, the universe would shrink; the bodies would come closer, increasing the net inward pull, and ultimately the universe would collapse onto itself. Newton's arguments against a static, finite universe were as eloquent as they were lucid:

> ... it seems to me that if the matter of our sun and planets, and all the matter of the universe, were evenly scattered throughout all the heavens, and every particle had an innate gravity toward all the rest, and the whole space, throughout which this matter was scattered, was but finite, the matter on the outside of the space would by its gravity tend toward all the matter on the inside, and by consequence fall down into the middle of the whole space, and there compose one great spherical mass. But if the matter was evenly disposed throughout an infinite space, it could never convene into one mass, but some of it would convene into one mass and some into another, so as to make an infinite number of great masses, scattered at great distances from one to another throughout all that infinite space.[22]

Newton's theoretical foundation led to a wider acceptance of the Copernican system although stellar parallax - the experimental confirmation of the revolution of the earth around the sun - was yet to be detected. It was finally observed by a German astronomer, Friedrich Bessel, in 1838, almost 300 years after *De Revolutionibus* was published, putting at rest all doubts about the Copernican system. The picture of universe that emerged after Newton had the sun at its centre. The earth and other planets revolved around the sun and some planets had their own moons. The stars lay at great distances stretching to infinity. If the universe was infinite, there could be no centre, yet the sun was placed at the centre of the universe.

Speed of Light is Absolute and Time is Relative

The Newtonian picture of the universe - static and infinite - prevailed for over two centuries. Beginning the spring of 1905, Albert Einstein submitted a set of four papers - known as *annus mirabilis* (the year of miracle) papers - to the reputed German journal of Physics *Annalen der physik,* which completely revolutionised our understanding of space, time, matter and light. Einstein postulated that light propagated with a definite speed - the speed of light in air is 2,99,700 km/second - regardless of the motion of the source. Imagine that you are standing on a road and a car is approaching towards you with a speed of 60 km/hour. Your measurement of the speed of the ray coming from headlight will still be 2,99,700 km/second. The same is not the case if a person in the approaching car throws a ball with speed of 80 km/hour. The observer on the ground will measure the speed of ball to be 140 km/hour and not 80 km/hour, that is, the speeds are added. But the speed of light is immune to the rule of addition. It should not be misconstrued that the speed of the car, being a negligible fraction of the speed of light, has been ignored during the addition. Even if the car was travelling at half the speed of light, the rays would still emanate from the headlight of the car with a speed of 299,700 km/second for an observer on the ground. The constancy of the speed of light has funny consequences - the time slows down if you are moving - and this can be better illustrated with an example.

Let us assume that a railcar is moving with a speed of 15 m/s rightward. An observer P standing on the extreme left of the car throws the ball towards the right with a speed of 20 m/s (assume frictionless surface). The ball travels to the other extreme of the car (10 m away), gets reflected with the same speed and comes back to P. P observes that the ball moves 10 m in half a second to hit the other end and the same on the return path. An observer Q on the ground finds the ball leaving with a speed of 35 m/s. It travels 17.5 m in half a second to hit the right end the car because the car has moved 7.5 m in the meantime. On the return journey, it moves only 2.5 m and reaches P in half a second. Both the observers agree on the time elapsed between the events. What will happen if the speeds are not added and the ball moves with a speed of 20 m/s for an observer on the ground regardless of the speed of the railcar? Q will observe that the ball takes 2 s to reach the right end and 0.3 s to return to P, that is, the time runs slowly in the moving car.

Now imagine P sending a light beam instead of a ball and a mirror at the right end of the car that reflects the beam back to P. Since the speed of light does not depend upon the motion of the source or the observer, time will run slowly in the car for an observer on the ground. Equally, for an observer in the car the time will run slowly on the ground because all motion is relative. However, the effect of time dilation is not noticeable in everyday life because the speed of even the fastest moving object is a very small fraction of the speed of light. The constancy of the speed of light also causes length contraction in the direction of the motion. Therefore, the length of the car will appear to be shorter to Q, an effect that has been ignored in the calculation for the sake of simplicity. It also puts an upper limit on the speed a material body can acquire because mass increases with increasing speed, and therefore it requires stronger force to further accelerate the object. Readers may ask why the time should be measured by sending a light pulse at all. Well, nothing in the universe travels faster than the light and it is the most universal entity in the cosmos. The occurrence of an event is recorded by an observer only when the light from the event reaches him.

Although time dilation is a logical consequence of the constancy of the speed of light, it is difficult to understand how an ordinary mechanical clock slows down while in motion. To understand this, let us assume two clocks, an ordinary mechanical clock and a light clock, being flown in a spacecraft at a very high speed, which were synchronized on the earth before the flight. If the light clock slows down but not the ordinary clock, an observer sitting in the spacecraft can measure its speed only by the difference in the readings of the two clocks, which violates the principle of physics: we cannot measure the speed of a train from inside without any reference to the outside world because motion is relative. All clocks are designed to measure time, but if time itself slows down, no matter which clock is used, they will all show the same time.

Einstein's Special Theory of Relativity discarded the notion of absolute space and time held by Newtonian mechanics. Two different observers moving with uniform velocity with respect to each other would not agree on the time interval between any two events, and the greater the relative velocity between them the greater would be the disagreement. Assume that a person is standing on the earth and the other is moving in a spaceship at a speed close to the speed of light. The observer on the ground is stationary in space but his time is ticking - 1, 2, 3, 4 ... and so on - whereas the person in the spaceship is traversing the space at great speed but is frozen in time. Faster one goes in space, slower is one's movement in time. Therefore, space and time do not exist independent of each other but are enmeshed together in what Einstein called space-time, ie, three dimensional space gets entangled with the fourth dimension of time. Of course, it is very hard to physically visualise such a four dimensional space-time.

Einstein Reconciles the Special Theory with Gravity

The special theory also came into conflict with Newtonian gravity. The universal law of gravitation, except for its inability to explain action at a distance, was a highly successful theory. It even predicted the existence of Neptune, the eighth planet in the solar system, before it was actually discovered. The earth is at a distance of about 150 million km from the sun and it traverses 30 km every second in its orbit around the sun. "In Newtonian gravity the sun keeps the earth in orbit with an unidentified gravitational tether that somehow instantaneously reaches across vast distances of space and grabs hold of the earth (and, similarly, the earth reaches out and grabs hold of the sun)."[23] In effect, the sun instantaneously sensed the change in the position of the earth. Einstein was rather uncomfortable with the idea that information could be exchanged at infinite speed, in violation of the upper limit of the speed imposed by the special theory. Therefore, he was looking for a theory that could reconcile the special theory with gravity.

Einstein did not have to wait too long. He made a serendipitous discovery one day when he was sitting in his patent office at Bern: A person freely falling towards the earth would find himself in a state of weightlessness.[24] Imagine an observer in an elevator, which is falling freely towards the earth. If he releases a ball downward, it will remain suspended in the air because both the observer and the ball are hurtling towards the earth with same acceleration. The observer cannot distinguish whether he is in zero gravity space or free fall by conducting any experiment within the elevator - this is called Einstein's Equivalence Principle. Let the observer throw a ball across the elevator, the ball will travel in a straight line and hit the opposite side of the elevator. However, to a person standing on the earth, the ball will appear to take a curved path because it not only moves across the elevator but also falls downward due to gravity. What happens if the observer sends a light beam across the elevator? By the same analogy, a person on the earth will observe the light beam take a curved path. Einstein was puzzled by the bending of light due to gravity - how could gravity attract light composed of massless particles. (It may be recalled that as per Newton's theory of gravitation a massless particle will not be attracted by any object howsoever heavy). Einstein further concluded that time slows down due to gravity. A clock at the surface of the earth ticks slower than one at the top of the mountain.

The Equivalence Principle laid the foundation of the General Theory of Relativity. From 1907 to 1915, Einstein worked on developing complex mathematics for depicting four dimensional space-time fabric. He showed that the space-time fabric is warped by the presence of mass. An object thrown upward from the earth falls back upon it not because of gravitational attractive force but due to the geometry of the space-time. Even light passing through a warped space-time would bend unlike Newtonian gravity. This is most commonly illustrated by imagining a stretched rubber sheet. Now if a heavy ball is placed in the middle of the sheet, a hemispherical depression will be formed, with the ball at its centre. Any small ball now rolled up from the centre will rise to some height, loose speed and come back. The greater the speed with which the ball is rolled up, higher it rises and at some critical speed it can escape the semi spherical bowl altogether. (Newtonian law had calculated the velocity to escape from the gravity of the earth to be 11.2 km/s.) Much like Newton's universal law of gravitation, Einstein's general theory also predicted an expanding or a contracting universe, but such was the dogma of static universe that Einstein modified his field equation by introducing a cosmological constant, which balanced the gravitational attraction at large distance and kept the universe static.

Einstein's General Theory explained how gravity works: matter warps space-time and space-time tells matter how to move. Newtonian dilemma of "action at a distance" - of two bodies acting upon each other over great distance without an agent – was resolved. In Newton's universe if the sun were to disappear suddenly, the earth would feel its absence instantaneously and, instead of orbiting the sun, move in a straight trajectory. In General Theory, the disappearance of the sun would cause warped space-time to flatten, but the ripple would reach the earth with the speed of light in eight minutes, and then the earth would move in a straight line in a flat space-time. The General Theory was elegant but there was no experimental confirmation as yet.

Mercury is the nearest planet to the sun and, therefore, its orbit is most elliptical, resembling an egg. Mercury orbits the sun once in 88 days, but strangely the orbit itself rotates around the sun – the point of closest approach of Mercury to the sun goes in a circle around it once in approximately 2,25,000 years (574 arc seconds per century). The calculation based on Newton's law of gravitation predicted a rotation of 531 arc seconds per century taking into account perturbation caused by nearby planets like Venus and the earth. The discrepancy of 43 arc seconds was explained by Einstein's field equations of the General Theory. Further confirmation of the General Theory came in 1919 when Arthur Eddington observed stars near the sun during total solar eclipse. The light coming from the stars was bent due to gravitational pull of the sun while passing near the sun causing their position to appear shifted.

Is the Milky Way the Only Galaxy in the Universe?

The general theory was a momentous achievement in science and had Einstein not introduced the cosmological constant in the field equation, it could have predicted that the universe was not only finite in size but also expanding. However, this did not deter the astronomers from attempting to measure the observable size of the universe. With better and more powerful telescopes, they peered deeper into the space, and each attempt pushed its frontier farther than before. The astronomers were also conscious of the presence of distant fuzzy objects in the sky called nebulae, which we now know as galaxies. In the early twentieth century, the size of the universe was estimated between 7,000 and 30,000 light years but Harlow Shapley, an American astronomer claimed that the universe was much larger than ever thought - 3,00,000 light years. Heber Curtis, a fellow astronomer, argued that the size of the Milky Way universe was not greater than 30,000 light years and spiral nebulae like Andromeda were separate 'island universes' not part of our system. The difference of opinion between the two astronomers led to the Great Debate, which was held on 26th April 1920 at the National Academy of Sciences in Washington. Shapely began on a philosophical note outlining the growing diminution of the position of mankind in the cosmos:

> The physical universe was anthropocentric to primitive man. At a subsequent stage of intellectual progress it was centred in a restricted area on the surface of the earth. Still later, to Ptolemy and his school, the universe was geocentric; but since the time of Copernicus the sun, as the dominating body of the solar system, has been considered to be at or near the centre of the stellar realm. With the origin of each of these successive conceptions, the system of stars has ever appeared larger than was thought before. Thus the significance of man and the earth in the sidereal scheme has dwindled with advancing knowledge of the physical world, and our conception of the dimensions of the discernible stellar universe has progressively changed. Is not further evolution of our ideas probable? In the face of great accumulations of new and relevant information can we firmly maintain our old cosmic conceptions?[25]

The Milky Way was a huge galaxy 3,00,000 light years in diameter and the sun was located at least 50,000 light years from the centre of the system, Shapely argued. He placed the farthest globular cluster at a distance of 2,20,000 light years. Today we know that he overestimated the size of our galaxy by a factor of three and since the farthest object was at a distance less than the size of the Milky Way, he concluded that it contained all objects including spiral nebulae. Curtis was more circumspect in relying upon the existing data of the distances to spiral nebulae as their estimates varied widely. According to his calculation, Andromeda spiral nebula was 5,00,000 light years away and by measuring its angular size he estimated that its size would be comparable to the Milky Way galaxy. He concluded "that the spirals are not intra-galactic objects but island universes, like our own galaxy, and that the spirals, as external galaxies, indicate to us a greater universe into which we may penetrate to distances of ten million to a hundred million light-years."[26] In the absence of sufficient data, the debate remained inconclusive with both sides claiming victory. However, only four years later, Edwin Hubble's calculation showed that Andromeda nebula was 9,30,000 light years away from the earth, far beyond the Milky Way, confirming Curtis's prediction. Shapely's question was answered, perhaps not in the way he had desired. Mankind was further marginalised in the grand scheme of the cosmos.

Readers may be wondering as to how astronomers calculate distances to extra-terrestrial objects that are thousands of light years away. The oldest method is parallax, which has been discussed earlier, but this is suitable only for stars located up to a distance of 400 light years because the parallax beyond that is too small to be detected. The colour of a star is a good indicator of its surface temperature - the higher the temperature, the greater the blue component in the spectrum of a star. The temperature, in turn, determines the intrinsic brightness (luminosity) of the star. The distance of the star is then calculated by comparing the intrinsic brightness with the apparent brightness of the star when seen from the earth. A star 20 light years away will appear four times dimmer than a star of the same intrinsic brightness at a distance of 10 light years. Stars are divided into seven groups according to their colour: O, B, A, F, G, K, and M, the temperature of O star being highest and M lowest.

Cepheid variable stars are a special type of stars whose brightness varies in a regular periodic manner. Typically, the brightness of such stars vary from low to high and again low within a period of 1 day to 100 days. Henrietta Swan Leavitt, an American astronomer investigated thousands of Cepheid stars and interestingly found that there was a direct relationship between their time period and luminosity. The time period of variable star can be easily calculated from the earth, which in turn gives the luminosity. Thereafter, the ratio of apparent and intrinsic brightness is used to determine the distance of the star. Hubble discovered Cepheid variable stars with the then largest 100 inch Hooker telescope at Mount Wilson Observatory, California in Andromeda nebula and employed this method to determine their distances from the earth.

Universe is Expanding

Hubble's calculation proved that the Milky Way galaxy was not alone in the universe and it actually might contain several galaxies. The stage was now set for yet another leap in astronomy, but to understand that a brief introduction to Doppler's work is necessary. Imagine you are standing in knee deep water in the sea and counting the number of wave crests that strike you. If you start moving into the sea on a speed boat, you will count a higher number of crests hitting you. The exact opposite will happen if you move from the deep sea towards the coast. It is for this reason that the whistle (sound wave) of an approaching train appears shriller to the ears than when it is moving away. If we move towards a wave-source, its frequency increases or wavelength decreases and vice versa. Visible light contains different colours from red (wavelength 750 nanometre) to violet (wavelength 380 nanometre), which can be seen by passing the sunlight through a prism. Since light also behaves like a wave, the wavelength of light from a source moving away from us appear to be elongated – this is known as Doppler effect. The magnitude of the shift in wavelength indicates the speed of the source or observer, that is, the greater the shift, the greater the speed.

The spectrum of light emanating from a star contains dark lines because certain wavelengths of light are absorbed by its constituent matters. While Vesto Slipher was studying the spectra of spiral nebulae, he observed that the dark lines (missing wavelengths) had shifted, which persuaded him to conclude that spiral nebulae were moving with respect to the earth. He measured the radial velocities of 41 spiral nebulae, 36 of which were found receding from the solar system and five approaching. The fastest nebula receding from the earth recorded a speed of 1,800 km per second.[27] But at that time it was not known that spiral nebulae were separate galaxies. Nor could any sense be made out of mixed results of the velocities of nebulae.

In 1927, Georges Lemaitre, a Belgian priest and cosmologist, in a remarkable paper in an obscure French journal first proposed that the universe was expanding. Lemaitre's solution of the field equation of Einstein yielded a homogeneous universe of constant mass and increasing radius. However, the paper was not translated into English until 1931, and before that Edwin Hubble, an American astronomer established a direct relationship between the distance of a galaxy and its outward velocity. Hubble plotted a graph of radial velocities of galaxies obtained by Slipher against their distances, which he had measured with the help of Cepheid stars. The graph turned out to be a straight line: the farther the galaxy, the faster it was moving away. Indeed, the universe was expanding. The ratio of galactic velocity and its distance came to be known as the Hubble constant, elegantly expressed in a simple equation, $v = H_0 \times d$. As per Hubble's calculation, its value was approximately 150 km/s per million light years. Therefore, a galaxy at a distance of one million light years away would be receding with a velocity of 150 km/s and one at distance of two million light years with a speed of 300 km/s. Later, the value of the constant was considerably reduced to 22 km/s per million light years upon discovery of significant errors in the original distance data.

If the universe was expanding, thought Lemaitre, earlier it must have been smaller in size and farther we went into the past, smaller it would be. Therefore, the universe would have been born at a definite time in the past from a single super-dense atom containing the entire mass:

> I would picture the evolution as follows: At the origin, all the mass of the universe would exist in the form of a unique atom; the radius of the universe, although not strictly zero, being relatively small. The whole universe would be produced by the disintegration of this primeval atom. It can be shown that the radius of space must increase. Some fragments retain their products of disintegration and form clusters of stars or individual stars of any mass.... Whether this is [a] wild imagination or [a] physical hypothesis cannot be said at present, but we may hope that the question will not wait too long to be solved.[28]

Fred Hoyle, a British astronomer, coined and popularized the term 'big bang' in radio talks in 1940s for the cataclysmic explosion that created the universe from a primeval atom. From this, it should not be inferred that he supported the big bang hypothesis; rather he propounded an alternative steady state hypothesis in which the universe had been in existence since eternity. The steady state hypothesis did not deny the expansion of the universe but contended that new matter was being created continuously and therefore the density of the universe at a very large scale remained constant. Hoyle argued that if matter could be created at the instant of big bang, nothing prevented its creation continuously. A universe with no beginning and no end was aesthetically pleasing; the big bang on the other hand smacked too much of an intervention by a Creator. Both the hypotheses remained in currency until 1965 when cosmic microwave radiation was detected, which eclipsed Hoyle's idea.

At the big bang, the universe was incredibly hot and it underwent rapid expansion at a speed greater than the speed of light. This does not violate Einstein's principle that nothing can travel faster than the light. Imagine a balloon with several dot marks on its surface. If it is blown up, its entire surface expands and the dots move away from one another. No matter where you stand on the surface of the balloon, the same phenomenon is observed, that is, there is no special location on its surface. The four dimensional space-time has been expanding in a similar manner since its birth. Of course, in the beginning there were no galaxies, they were formed much later. The universe was a hot soup of plasma consisting of protons, neutrons, electrons and photons. The photons were continuously scattered by the protons and electrons in the dense soup and therefore they remained trapped within a very narrow region around the place where they were created. After approximately 3,80,000 years from the big bang, protons captured electrons to form neutral atoms. The universe became sparser and the photons interacted less with the matter, which allowed the photons to leave their place of birth and travel far and wide in the universe.

The early photons emitted from different points in the universe spread in all directions. Arno Allan Penzias and Robert Woodrow Wilson, both American astronomers, detected these photons with radio telescope in 1964 at Bell Laboratories. Since our galaxy is receding at a very high speed with respect to the point from where these photons were emitted, their wavelength has increased (Doppler Effect) so much that they cannot be seen by human eyes. Penzias and Wilson accidently discovered these photons and found that they were coming uniformly from all directions, which convinced them that they were indeed looking at the afterglow from the early universe. (When we look at a galaxy say 5 billion light years away, it means that the light we see now had left the galaxy 5 billion years ago.) The big bang hypothesis was experimentally confirmed.

We have come a long way from the stationary earth to an expanding universe that began at the big bang. So let us now look at the position of the earth in the cosmos. It is spinning on its axis with a speed of 0.46 km/s at the equator while it revolves around the sun with a speed of 30 km/s. The sun is approximately 30,000 light years from the centre of the Milky Way - which is 1,00,000 light years across - going around it once in 225 million years with an orbital speed of 225 km/s. Our nearest neighbour Andromeda galaxy is 2.54 million light years away from the earth and it is likely to collide with the Milky Way in four billion years. Andromeda and the Milky Way are part of Virgo Cluster, containing 1,000 to 2,000 galaxies. Although space-time is expanding and galaxies are flying apart, the gravitational attraction between Andromeda and the Milky Way is strong enough to pull each towards the other. The universe contains approximately 200 billion galaxies, each having billions of stars. Its age is estimated to be 13.8 billion years and the size, 92 billion light years.

If the universe were of the size of the earth, the earth's size would reduce to one hundred thousandth of a hydrogen atom. If the age of the universe were equal to the average human life span, we would live only for 15 seconds. We find ourselves not at the centre but tucked in a remote corner, not stationary but moving with great speed that we never experience, and our significance - and indeed vanity - has been reduced nearly to zero. How far our understanding has changed since we thought ourselves to be at the centre of the universe!

Universe in the *Vedas*

In the finest tradition of Hindu philosophy, *Nasadiya Sukta*, the creation hymn in *Rig Veda* begins on a sceptical note, reflecting its characteristic ambiguity. *Sat* means which exists and *Asat* means which does not exist, non-existent. *Nasadiya* combines together two words *na* (not) and *asat* (non-existent), therefore it is double negative, one which is not non-existent:

> Then even nothingness was not, nor existence,
> There was no air then, nor the heavens beyond it.
> What covered it? Where was it? In whose keeping?
> Was there then cosmic water, in depths unfathomed?
>
> Then there were neither death nor immortality,
> nor was there then the torch of night and day,
> The One breathed windlessly and self-sustaining.
> There was that One then, and there was no other.[29]

Space and time are the properties of the universe; they came into being at the big bang. Therefore, the notion of existence before the big bang is absurd, and since non-existence is defined as a binary of existence, it is equally meaningless to think that non-existence existed before the creation of the universe. *Rig Veda* asserts that there was neither existence nor non-existence before the creation of the universe:

> At first there was only darkness wrapped in darkness,
> All this was only unillumined water.
> That One which came to be, enclosed in nothing,
> arose at last, born of the power of heat ...

But, after all, who knows, and who can say
whence it all came, and how creation happened?
The gods themselves are later than creation,
so who knows truly whence it has arisen?

Whence all creation had its origin,
he, whether he fashioned it or whether he did not,
he, who surveys it all from highest heaven,
he knows - or maybe even he does not know.[30]

It further speculates that the universe was created by the power of the heat, perhaps an explosion and ends with asking more questions than providing definite answers. It even doubts whether the God himself knows about the creation of the universe. Later, Hindus developed a very elaborate and intricate cyclic concept of the Cosmos, one that has been in existence since eternity and that will exist forever, but not without getting created and destroyed repeatedly. In the Holy trinity of Hinduism, Brahma is the Creator, Vishnu, the Preserver and the Shiva, the Destroyer. When 4.32 billion years elapse in the Cosmos, one day in the life of Brahma is spent. Thereafter, the Cosmos is destroyed by Shiva and Brahma goes to sleep for a night, which lasts for another 4.32 billion years. As Brahma day breaks, he recreates the Cosmos again. "The Hindu religion is the only one of the world's great faiths dedicated to the idea that the Cosmos undergoes an immense, indeed an infinite, number of deaths and rebirths. It is the only religion in which the time scales correspond, no doubt by accident, to those of modern scientific cosmology. Its cycles run from our ordinary day and night to a day and night of Brahma, 8.64 billion years long, longer than the age of the Earth or the Sun and about half the time since the Big Bang."[31] The creation-destruction cycle continues for 100 Brahma years, at the end of which Brahma himself is destroyed. We are currently supposed to be in the 51st Brahma year, that is, 155.52 trillion years have elapsed since the birth of

Brahma – a scale of time that has not been conceived anywhere else.

Any origin of universe hypothesis either requires a Creator or an assumption that it was a causeless event. The former immediately raises a question: who created the Creator and the latter negates the natural established order of things in the universe in which every effect is preceded by a cause. *Puranas* contain different stories about the origin of Brahma, Vishnu and Shiva, claiming one of them to be *swayambhu*, that is, self-manifested, a causeless being. Science too is confronted with the same problem because it cannot tell what happened at the Big Bang, let alone what preceded it. At the moment of Big Bang all mathematical equations break down and no scientific investigation is possible. Since the concept of space-time originated at the Big Bang, it is, scientists contend, meaningless to talk of anything before it. "... we may have to get used to the idea of an absolute zero of time – a moment in the past beyond which it is in principle impossible to trace any chain of cause and effect. The question is open, and may always remain open."[32] However, science's inability to probe the big bang – and anything before it – cannot be a proof for non-existence of existence in some other unknown form.

Science should not be a place for dogma but history is replete with instances when dogma has prevailed, almost like a religious belief, even in the face of overwhelming evidence. Scientists indeed have challenged many dogmas and yet surprisingly they have succumbed to others. Copernicus was brave in bringing the sun to the centre of the universe but clung on to circular orbit as the perfect path of movement. Newton discovered the universal law of gravitation, which should ideally have led to a universe that was not static. Einstein's equations yielded an expanding universe but he neutralized the result by introducing a cosmological constant in the equation, only to regret later when Hubble's seminal paper transformed our view in a very fundamental way.

Fate of the Universe

The big bang hypothesis was a natural corollary of an expanding universe, later substantiated by the discovery of cosmic microwave radiation. It sealed the debate on the origin of the universe but there were two views on its ultimate fate. If the universe contained mass above a critical level, the gravitational attraction between them would slow down and ultimately stop the expansion. The universe, thereafter, would start collapsing and end in a big crunch – opposite of the big bang. If the mass was below the critical level, the universe would continue expanding forever, albeit at a slower and slower rate, but the expansion would never cease altogether. Therefore, finding the total mass of the universe could provide clue to its fate. Scientists believed that the distribution of mass in the universe was homogeneous. There could indeed be local variation in distribution but if a sufficiently large region of the universe was chosen and its mass was estimated, the same could be extrapolated to determine the mass of the entire universe. When scientists used this method to estimate the mass of the entire universe, they were surprised to find that it was far below the critical level required to halt the expansion of the universe. Was some other type of matter present in the universe?

Although 'dark matter' was hypothesized way back in the 1930s, it took almost forty years to substantiate its existence. Since it does not interact with light or any form of electromagnetic radiation, it cannot be seen and its presence is felt only by the gravitational force that it exerts on ordinary matter. Vera Rubin, an American astronomer, was studying the Andromeda galaxy when she found that luminous mass (mass that interacts with light) present in the galaxy was not sufficient to hold the galaxy together because the stars were rotating so fast that they would fly off at that speed. Rubin concluded that the galaxy contained a large quantity of dark matter which held it together. Later scientific developments reaffirmed her contention and it is now known that the total quantity of dark matter far exceeds the luminous matter in the universe.

The total quantity of matter, both luminous and dark, present in the universe is not sufficient to halt its expansion but the universe must at least exhibit signs of slowing down because of gravitational attraction between matter. In the 1990s, two groups were independently searching for this evidence: Supernova Cosmology Project was led by Saul Perlmutter at Lawrence Berkeley National Laboratory and High-Z Supernova Search Team by Brian Schmidt at Australian National University. In Hubble's equation, $v=H_0 \times d$, if Hubble parameter H_0 remains constant over time, the expansion of the universe would accelerate. Assume that a galaxy is at a distance of 1 billion light years from the earth and therefore it would be receding with a velocity of 22,000 km per second. In next one billion years, the galaxy would be further away from the earth by approximately 75 million light years and therefore its velocity would increase to 23,600 km per second as per Hubble's equation. However, if Hubble parameter decreases over time, two situations may emerge: if it decreases more rapidly than galaxies move apart, the recessional velocity will decrease with time, that is, the expansion of the universe will slow down. If, on the other hand, the Hubble parameter decreases but slowly, the expansion will speed up. The two groups were looking for the evidence of slowing down of expansion of the universe; instead, to their utter surprise and dismay, they discovered that it was actually speeding up.

The initial speed that was imparted to the constituents of the universe at the big bang should ideally have decreased with time. The accelerating universe, therefore, presented a new paradox to the scientists: What mysterious force is speeding it up? It is now hypothesized that 'dark energy', which permeates the entire universe, is responsible for the acceleration of the universe. While gravity pulls objects towards one another, dark energy does the opposite - it pushes things apart. If galaxies are gaining speed, this mysterious form of energy must be getting created continuously. But there are many questions which remain unanswered: What is its source? Is dark energy an intrinsic property of space? Is it a type of repulsive force? If little is known about dark matter, even less is known about dark energy as it remains completely shrouded in mystery. And since ordinary matter comprises less than five percent of the universe, the fate of the universe will not be known until we unravel the mystery of dark matter and dark energy.

Our understanding of the universe has increased in the last two millennia, yet so much remains to be known that we look at the universe with the same feeling of bewilderment as our forefathers did. We do not know what the fate of the universe is. We do not know how exactly it came into existence as the moment of big bang is a singularity where all equations collapse. We cannot even reach very close to it because, as we shall later see, the physics of small scale (quantum physics) and the physics of large scale (general theory of relativity) have not been united and we do not know how gravity behaves at quantum scale. The discovery of accelerating universe has forced us to ponder whether we have understood gravity in its fullness. Of course, anything before the big bang is absolutely beyond the realm of science, at least at present. Towards the very end of a long, gruelling journey, when one quietly anticipates the satisfaction of having reached, but instead finds that there is still a long way to go, even a brave scientist can throw his hands up in exasperation that "the more the universe seems comprehensible, the more it also seems pointless."[33]

Notes and References

1. *On the Heavens by Aristotle,* translated by WKC Guthrie, p 253, Harvard University Press, London, 1939.
2. *Ibid.*
3. *The Aryabhatiya of Aryabhata: An Ancient Indian Work on Mathematics and Astronomy,* translated by Walter Eugene Clark, p 28, The University of Chicago Press, 1930.
4. *Ibid,* p 64.
5. "Aryabhata I, His Life and His Contributions", SM Razaullah Ansari, *Bulletin of the Astronomical Society of India,* Vol 5, 1977, pp 10-18.
6. "Modification of the Earlier Indian Planetary Theory by the Kerala Astronomers (c 1500 AD) and the Implied Heliocentric Picture of Planetary Motion", K Ramasubramanian, MD Srinivas and MS Sriram, *Current Science,* Vol 66, No 10, 1994, pp 784-90.
7. *Nicholas Copernicus on the Revolutions,* Vol 2, edited by Jerzy Dobrzycki, translation and commentary by Edward Rosen, p 22, The Macmillan Press Ltd, London, 1978.
8. *Ibid,* p 3.
9. *God's Planet* by Owen Gingerich, p 24, Harvard University Press, Cambridge, 2014.
10. "As quoted in Tycho Brahe's Critique of Copernicus and the Copernican System", Ann Blair, *Journal of the History of Ideas,* Vol 51, No 3, 1990, p 364.
11. *Ibid,* p 365.
12. "Truth in Science: Proof, Persuasion, and the Galileo Affair", Owen Gingerich, *Perspectives on Science and Christian Faith,* Vol 55, No 2, 2003, p 82.
13. "Tycho Brahe's Critique of Copernicus and the Copernican System", Ann Blair, *Journal of the History of Ideas,* Vol 51, No 3, 1990, p 365.
14. "Truth in Science: Proof, Persuasion, and the Galileo Affair",

Owen Gingerich, *Perspectives on Science and Christian Faith,* Vol 55, No 2, 2003, p 82.

15. *Tycho Brahe: A Picture of Scientific Life and Work in the Sixteenth Century* by John Louis Emil Dreyer, p 180, Cambridge University Press, 2014.
16. *Johannes Kepler and the New Astronomy* by James R Voelkel, pp 48-57, Oxford University Press, New York, 1999.
17. *The Essential Galileo,* edited and translated by Maurice A Finocchiaro, p 177, Hackett Publishing Company, Inc, Indianapolis, 2008.
18. *Mathematical Principles of Natural Philosophy by Sir Isaac Newton,* p 83, translated by Andrew Motte, First American edition, Daniel Adee, New York, 1848.
19. *Ibid,* pp 74-75.
20. *Sir Isaac Newton's Mathematical Principles of Natural Philosophy and His System of the World,* Vol 2, Motte's translation revised by Florian Cajori, p 634, University of California Press, Los Angeles, 1934.
21. *Nicholas Copernicus on the Revolutions,* Vol 2, edited by Jerzy Dobrzycki, translated and commentary by Edward Rosen, pp 18-20, The Macmillan Press Ltd, London, 1978.
22. *Four Letters from Sir Isaac Newton to Doctor Bentley Containing Some Arguments in Proof of a Deity,* pp 2-3, London, printed for R & J Dodsley, Pall-Mall, 1756.
23. *The Elegant Universe: Superstrings, Hidden Dimensions, and the Quest for the Ultimate Theory* by Brian Greene, p 67, Vintage, London, 2000.
24. "An Old Man's Toy" by A Zee in *E = Einstein: His Life, His Thought, and His Influence on Our Culture,* edited by Donald Goldsmith and Marcia Bartusiak, p 224, Sterling, New York, 2006.
25. "The Scale of the Universe", Harlow Shapely and Heber Curtis, *Bulletin of the National Research Council,* Vol 2, Part 3, No 11, May 1921, pp 171-2.
26. *Ibid,* p 217.
27. *The Mathematical Theory of Relativity* by Arthur Eddington, p 162, Cambridge University Press, 1960.
28. As quoted in *Archives of the Universe: 100 Discoveries that Transformed Our Understanding of the Cosmos,* edited by Marcia Bartusiak, p 324, Vintage Books, New York, 2006.

29. As quoted in *The Wonder that was India* by AL Basham, p 249, Rupa & Co, New Delhi, 1989.
30. *Ibid*, p 250.
31. *Cosmos* by Carl Sagan, pp 213-4, Ballantine Books, New York, 1980.
32. *The First Three Minutes: A Modern View of the Origin of the Universe* by Steven Weinberg, p 149, Basic Books, New York, 1993.
33. *Ibid*, p 154.

2

Is the Search for Immortality Futile?

> Many, I doubt not, will think that attempting gravely to convert so absurd a paradox as the immortality of men on earth, or indeed, even the perfectibility of man in society, is a waste of time and words; and that such unfounded conjectures are best answered by neglect.
>
> – *Thomas Malthus*

> If you were to destroy in mankind the belief in immortality, not only love but every living force maintaining the life of the world would at once be dried up. – *Fyodor Dostoevsky*

The human desire to live forever has existed for centuries even though such a possibility seems no less remote today than it was anytime earlier despite rapid advancement in biological sciences. The idea of elixir, a secret formulation for maintaining eternal youth and defying death, is found in many ancient civilisations like Indian, Chinese and Greek. Greeks called it *ambrosia* and *nectar*, Chinese called it *pinyin* – peaches of immortality – and Indians, *amrit*. Legend has it that sage Durvasa on his way back from the heaven met Lord Indra, who was sitting on his elephant, Airawat. Durvasa offered a garland to Indra as a gesture of respect, but he paid no attention and instead threw the garland on the elephant's head. It fell down on the ground and was trampled by the elephant. Enraged, sage Durvasa cursed Indra that he would lose all his power and glory. Thus, the authority of Indra declined and the devils (*asuras*) started ruling the heaven, forcing Indra to seek advice from Brahma to defeat the devils. Brahma then suggested that the ocean of milk should be churned to obtain *amrit*, consuming which will make the gods immortal. Brahma also told the gods that the churning of ocean could not be done without the help of *asuras*. Thus, the gods and the devils together churned the ocean of milk which yielded a pitcher of *amrit*. A fierce battle between the gods and the devils ensued for the control of nectar, but the gods fraudulently deprived the devils from getting *amrit* and became immortal.

The myth of *amrit* is a powerful tale that confronts eternal questions - the questions that emerge almost as soon as we become aware of the temporariness of our existence. Animals like chimpanzee and elephants have been found to display emotions at the demise of their family members or companions. But it is difficult to tell whether they are conscious of their own death in the way a human is aware that his existence in the universe will come to an end one day, and therefore he cannot resist asking questions: How did life originate? Why are there so many different species? Who am I? Where I have come from? What is my place in the universe? What happens after death? If we were to become immortal, the anxiety about our place in the universe would cease to exist. It is only natural, therefore, that humanity has been gripped by this desire. But will it be possible for us to live forever defying old age and death? Is it even desirable?

Life Emerges Spontaneously from Decaying Matter

Before the advent of modern science, it was widely believed that some form of life was generated spontaneously from non-living matter - particularly from decaying matter. "Anyone could see that flies and maggots arose from rotting meat, frogs from swamps, mice from moist grain. Nearly everyone believed that spontaneous generation of life was not only possible, but common among the simple - so called lower - plants and animals."[1] People, of course, knew through simple observation that more complex form of life was created by reproduction. Francesco Redi, an Italian physician, naturalist, and poet, challenged the theory of spontaneous generation by conducting a series of experiments, which he published in a book *Experiments on the Generation of Insects* (*Esperienze Intorno alla Generazione degl'Insetti*) in 1668. Redi attributed the mind boggling variety of species found on the earth to the Creator and asserted that life thereafter was created only by reproduction:

> I shall express my belief that the Earth, after having brought forth the first plants and animals at the beginning by the order of the ... Creator, has never since produced any kind of plants and animals ... and everything which we know in past or present times that she has produced came solely from the true seeds of the plants and animals themselves, which thus ... preserve their species. And, although it be a matter of daily observation that infinite numbers of worms are produced in dead bodies and decayed plants, I feel ... inclined to believe that ... the putrefied matter in which they are found has no other office than that of serving as a place ... where animals deposit their eggs at the breeding season, and in which they also find nourishment; otherwise, I assert that nothing is ever generated therein.[2]

Redi obtained a doctorate in medicine from the University of Pisa, where the other great Italian scientist, Galileo Galilei had also enrolled as a medical student, but later shifted to mathematics and natural philosophy. Redi's experiment was quite simple: He kept fresh meat in two sets of glass jars, one set covered and the other open. The open jars became full of maggots after sometime, but no maggots were observed in the closed jars. He concluded that maggots in the open jars developed from the eggs laid by the flies and not because of 'spontaneous generation'.

His conclusion was open to criticism on the ground that it was the absence of air that prevented spontaneous generation of maggots in the closed jars. Therefore, he improvised the experiment by covering the jars with gauze so as not to prevent the air from entering the jars, but maggots did not appear.[3]

Nevertheless, the controversy over spontaneous generation did not cease. The belief in the theory was too entrenched to be shaken up by a single experiment. Meanwhile, the use of microscopes in scientific experimentation was increasing and microorganisms, not visible to the naked eyes, were discovered, about which we will discuss later. Therefore, it was natural for the supporters of spontaneous generation to assume that although more complex form of life like maggots might not emerge from non-living matter, microorganisms could still be created spontaneously from non-living matter. "In 1748 ... John Needham and Georges Buffon boiled a quantity of mutton broth and then sealed it up in glass containers. Supposedly, the heat would kill any microorganisms that had been present in the broth initially. But when the glass containers were opened a few days later, rich colonies of microorganism were observed through the microscope."[4] The theory of spontaneous generation was back in currency.

In 1768, exactly one hundred years after the publication of Redi's *Experiments on the Generation of Insects*, another Italian biologist, Lazzaro Spallanzani refuted Needham's claim by arguing that he had not sufficiently heated the broth to kill all microorganisms present in the broth. Spallanzani repeated the experiment conducted by Needham but by heating the broth for about forty five minutes, and he found no trace of any microorganism, but the proponents of spontaneous generation remained far from convinced. They reasoned that heating the broth not only killed the microorganisms but also the vital life force present in the air, so essential for the sprouting of life.[5] Thus, the efforts of two

Italian scientists spread over a century could not conclusively refute 'spontaneous generation'.

Pouchet Spars with Pasteur Over Spontaneous Generation

Towards the middle of the 19th century, the dispute over 'spontaneous generation' had shifted to France, where Felix Pouchet, the Director of Rouen Museum of Natural History of France sparred with a young chemist and microbiologist, Louis Pasteur, rekindling the famous Needham-Spallanzani spat. Felix Pouchet boiled water in a flask and sealed it. The sealed flask was then kept in a mercury container upside down. The flask was unsealed, but the water remained inside the flask because mercury is heavier than water. Pouchet produced oxygen through chemical reaction to ensure that it was free from atmospheric contamination and passed this oxygen through a glass tube in the flask. As the gas went into the flask, it displaced water, and when the flask was half full of oxygen, he placed a small amount of carefully sterilised hay from below the surface of mercury into the flask. After a few days the hay broth was full of microorganisms. Pouchet took great care to ensure that microorganisms did not enter his experimental set up from outside, but despite this they grew in the hay broth, which led Pouchet to conclude that spontaneous generation did take place. He published his arguments in the favour of spontaneous generation in a book *Heterogenesis: A Treatise on Spontaneous Generation* in 1859.

Pouchet's experiment did not end the raging controversy over spontaneous generation and therefore the French Academy of Science established a 2,500 francs Alhumbert Prize in 1860 to conclusively resolve the debate once for all.[6] Although Pouchet and Pasteur stood on opposite ends of the divide, the principle behind their experiments was the same. Both heated one or other type of broth so as to kill any microorganism present in them and both tried to eliminate any contamination of the broth with microorganisms imported from the environment, but while Pouchet demonstrated that microorganisms grew in spite of that in the broth, Pasteur showed exactly the opposite.

Louis Pasteur poured some broth in a flask and bent its neck into a long drawn swan shape. The broth was heated to kill all existing germs and then was left to cool, but it remained sterile even after days and months. He repeated the experiment without the swan shaped neck only to find the broth teeming with microbes only after a few days. Pasteur argued that dust was trapped in the bend of swan shaped neck of the flask and therefore it could not travel against the gravity into the flask, preventing the broth from getting contaminated with microbes. Pasteur had earlier demonstrated that the air is full of dust motes and these motes almost always carry microbes. Addressing the crème de la crème of French society at the Sorbonne Scientific Soiree on 7th April 1864, Louis Pasteur systematically dismantled the arguments advanced by Pouchet:

> A beam of light from the stage will allow you to see that this room is full of dusts, which should not be trivialized, for sometimes they carry the germs of disease and death.... As for Pouchet, he has apparently eliminated the dusts by using oxygen gas and artificial air, and destroyed, by boiling, any germs that may be in the water or the hay. But he has not removed the dusts at the surface of the mercury, which carries the germs of the atmosphere into the flasks.[7]

Pasteur not only received the 2,500 francs Alhumbert Prize but also rightfully claimed that "never will the doctrine of spontaneous generation recover from the mortal blow struck by this simple experiment."[8] For close to 200 years - from Redi's experiment in 1668 to Pasteur's lecture in 1864 - biologists grappled with one of the most fundamental question about the origin of life, much in the same manner as physicists - from 1690 when Huygens proposed the wave theory of light to Einstein's photoelectric effect in 1905 - struggled to define the true nature of light.

Discovery of Cell

Meanwhile, a parallel development was taking place in biological sciences. Robert Hooke, an English scientist, observed various objects like the tip of a needle, the sting of a bee, the wings of flies etc under a compound microscope, which he had assembled himself. He published the details of the observations with accurate drawings in *Micrographia or Some Physiological Descriptions of Minute Bodies Made by Magnifying Glasses* in 1665, the year in which the great plague claimed several thousand lives in London. While Hooke was studying a good clear slice of cork under the microscope, he discovered empty spaces contained by walls much like a honeycomb, which he called cells. He estimated that one cubic inch of cork contained 1.26 billion cells.[9] As the cork cells were dead, Hooke could only see the cell walls and the space trapped within them, but it was not long before single-celled organisms were discovered.

Antonie van Leeuwenhoek was born in Delft, Holland in 1632 and his father passed away when he was only five years old. At the age of 16, Leeuwenhoek became an apprentice at a linen draper's shop in Amsterdam. A few years later in 1654, he came back to his home town to set up a drapery business of his own. He required powerful magnifying glasses to observe the quality of fabrics, which were simply not available, and therefore he was drawn to lens making. Robert Hooke's compound microscope, with which he had observed dead cork cells, provided a magnification of 20 to 50, whereas Leeuwenhoek made simple microscopes with one lens capable of magnifying objects 200 times.[10] Much like Hooke, Leeuwenhoek also had passion for studying various things under the microscope. He shared the details with his friend and physician Regnier de Graaf, who introduced his work to the Royal Society of London, which was formed in

1660 to promote the knowledge of the natural world through observation and experiment, and whose first Curator of Experiment was none other than Robert Hooke. Leeuwenhoek wrote more than 400 letters to the Royal Society from 1673 to his death in 1723 describing in great detail his observations, which also contained discovery of protozoa, bacteria, sperm cells, red blood cells, unicellular algae and unicellular fungi. He called these microbes animalcules – little animals; their modern names are of later origin. Leeuwenhoek reported the discovery of bacteria and also provided their precise drawings in the letter dated 17th September 1683:

> Though my teeth are kept usually very clean, nevertheless when I view them in a magnifying glass, I find growing between them a little white matter as thick as wetted flour: in this substance though I could not perceive any motion, I judged there might probably be living creatures.... I therefore took some of this flour and mixed it either with pure rainwater wherein were no animals; or else with some of my spittle and then to my great surprise perceived that the aforesaid matter contained very many small living animals, which moved themselves very extravagantly. The biggest sort had the shape of A. Their motion was strong and nimble, and they darted themselves through the water or spittle, as a Jack or Pike does through the water.[11]

A person without any formal university education, who knew no language other than Dutch, came to be known as the father of microbiology for the discovery of single-celled organisms, and because of which all forms of life – from as simple as bacteria to as complex as mammals – became known to mankind. Thereafter, the world had to wait for over 150 years for the next big breakthrough that enhanced our understanding of life when a German botanist, Matthias Schleiden proposed that all plants consisted of cells in 1838. In the following year, a German zoologist, Theodor Schwann extended the proposition to animals by arguing that "all organized bodies are composed of essentially similar parts, namely, of cells; that these cells are formed and grow in accordance with essentially similar laws; and, therefore, that these processes must, in every instance, be produced by the same powers."[12] Schleiden and Schwann laid down two of the three postulates of the cell theory: all organisms are composed of one or more cells and cell is the basic unit of life. However, Schwann wrongly assumed that "the formation of cells bears the same relation to organic nature that crystallization does to inorganic."[13] In other words, Schwann believed that cells were created spontaneously from non-cellular matter, a view that was prevalent in those times, and which has been discussed earlier.

The statement "all cells come from cells" is usually attributed to the German zoologist Rudolf Virchow, but the idea was first advanced by fellow German Robert Remak while he was studying the growth of frog embryo in 1852.[14] Virchow firmly put his weight behind the idea and popularized it through the simple dictum – *omnis cellula a cellula*. The cell theory was now complete. All organisms, simple or complex, consist of one or more cells. In more complex organisms like human beings, a group of cells combine to form tissue and a group of tissues form an organ to perform a specialized function. The cell has all the attributes of life: it produces energy, grows, responds to external environment, reproduces etc. And finally, cells arise only from the division of existing cells.

Our existence begins with a single cell, when a sperm cell hits an ovum cell and forms a zygote. The zygote divides itself into two, and then two cells become four, eight and so on and so forth. New cells are created and the old cells die all the time. In the beginning, the rate of cell division exceeds the rate of cell death, which is essential for the body to grow, but eventually the two processes balance each other. A fully grown human body has 30 trillion cells and if all cells that are formed during the entire life span are counted, they add up to staggering 10,000 trillion.[15] A simple calculation will show that the astounding figure of 10,000 trillion is reached by a cell dividing itself 53 times and no more.

Remak's observation - all cells come from cells - and Pasteur's convincing repudiation of spontaneous generation 12 years later left no doubt that all organisms, whether simple or complex, were produced from the division of existing cells. Therefore, the fundamental question that begged an answer was: How did millions of species come into existence? The theological view was that in the beginning all species were created by God and after that they were left to replicate according to natural laws, but science, despite its reservations, had no credible explanation to offer for the origin of different species.

Darwin Proposes the Theory of Evolution

It was in this historical context that Charles Darwin proposed the theory of evolution in 1859, which is arguably the most controversial scientific theory ever, admired and reviled in equal measure. Its line of reasoning is so engaging and unimpeachable, but the conclusion is so difficult to accept despite its profound simplicity that a large number of people are ill at ease with it even now. Darwin had anticipated the furore that would be caused by the theory and therefore he had waited for years to burnish the arguments. Ultimately, he published *On the Origin of Species* in 1859 after much prodding from his Scottish geologist friend Charles Lyell and alarmed by the letter from Alfred Russel Wallace in the summer of 1858 - who was at that time exploring the Malay archipelago - which indicated that he was independently developing the same theory.[16] Darwin valiantly confronted objections to the theory of evolution but remained steadfast in his conclusion:

> That many and serious objections may be advanced against the theory of descent with modification through variation

> and natural selection, I do not deny. I have endeavoured to give to them their full force. Nothing at first can appear more difficult to believe than that the more complex organs and instincts have been perfected, not by means superior to, though analogous with, human reason, but by the accumulation of innumerable slight variations, each good for the individual possessor. Nevertheless, this difficulty, though appearing to our imagination insuperably great, cannot be considered real if we admit the following propositions, namely, that all parts of the organisation and instincts offer, at least, individual differences – that there is a struggle for existence leading to the preservation of profitable deviations of structure or instinct – and, lastly, that gradations in the state of perfection of each organ may have existed, each good of its kind. The truth of these propositions cannot, I think, be disputed.[17]

Darwin's proposition that complex form of life was created through the process of natural selection and not through divine intervention was an affront to the religious belief that every species was individually created by God. Ironically, Darwin did not deny the role of the divine in creating few initial forms of life from which complex species evolved:

> It is interesting to contemplate a tangled bank, clothed with many plants of many kinds, with birds singing on the bushes, with various insects flitting about, and with worms crawling through the damp earth, and to reflect that these elaborately constructed forms, so different from each other, and dependent upon each other in so complex a manner, have all been produced by laws acting around us.... Thus, from the war of nature, from famine and death, the most exalted object which we are capable of conceiving, namely, the production of the higher animals, directly follows. There is grandeur in this view of life, with its several powers, having been originally breathed by the Creator into a few forms or into one; and that, whilst this planet has gone cycling on according to the fixed law of gravity, from so

> simple a beginning endless forms most beautiful and most wonderful have been, and are being evolved.[18]

Darwin observed different species inhabiting South America during his voyage on HMS Beagle and collected a huge amount of data, but the idea of natural selection as the mechanism for the evolution of species struck Darwin in 1838 while he was reading *An Essay on the Principle of Population*, in which Thomas Malthus argued that population increased in a geometrical ratio whereas subsistence in an arithmetic ratio.[19] Malthus further asserted that all plants and animals were affected by this restrictive law of nature. Darwin thought that the scarcity of necessities for the survival led to struggle for existence among the members of a species. Some members of a species developed special physical or behavioural traits to better adapt to its environment in order to increase its chance of survival. These traits were passed on to their offspring and slight variations accumulated over generations created a different species. Natural selection is the heart of Darwin's theory, which distinguishes it from earlier theories of evolution, notably by his grandfather Erasmus Darwin and French naturalist Jean Baptiste Lamarck.

The age of the earth is presently estimated to be 4.5 billion years but at the time of Darwin radiometric dating to ascertain the age of fossils was not invented. The earth was supposed to be not more than few to several thousand years old, which was not long enough for the slow process of evolution to create the varieties of species that existed on the earth. Darwin had read Charles Lyell's *Principles of Geology* during his voyage on HMS Beagle. Lyell's premise that geological action had shaped the earth over a very long period of time provided a crucial lead to Darwin and convinced him of the immense antiquity of the earth. He was tempted to estimate the age of the earth on the basis of denudation of Weald valley in the south of England, which he thought to have taken place due to marine erosion.

He arrived at a figure of 30,66,62,400 (approximately three hundred million) years on the basis of certain simple assumptions. The first edition of the *Origin* published in November 1859 carried the estimate, but it was severely criticised for being simplistic, unscientific and even speculative. Unable to defend the premise of calculation with credible arguments, Darwin removed all references to the age of the earth in the third edition of the *Origin* published in April 1861, but never lost confidence that time would validate his assumption, which ultimately proved to be prescient.[20]

Darwinism faced a more formidable challenge: The theory of natural selection required that special traits acquired by an organism due to adaptation be passed onto their offspring over generations so that minor variations accumulated over millions of years could give rise to a different species. Although inheritance was not properly understood in those times, it was commonly accepted that the characteristics of parents got blended in their offspring – and Darwin believed in the hypothesis of blending inheritance. Blending inheritance hypothesis implied that the traits of parents were averaged out in their offspring. If a tall person married a short person, the children would be expected to be of average height. This created a serious problem for evolution because the acquired traits by a member of species would be diluted in successive generations, and would not accrete as suggested by Darwin, leaving little opportunity for natural selection to work. Imagine a drop of milk being poured in a bucket of water; it will quickly dissolve in water, leaving little trace of it. Not surprisingly, evolution was attacked by Fleeming Jenkin, a Scottish engineer, in June 1867 in a paper published in the *North British Review* – a publication now extinct – for being inconsistent with blending inheritance.

> Suppose a white man to have been wrecked on an island inhabited by Negroes, and to have established himself in

> friendly relations with a powerful tribe, whose customs he has learnt. Suppose him to possess the physical strength, energy, and ability of a dominant white race, and let the food and climate of the island suit his constitution; grant him every advantage which we can conceive a white to possess over the native; concede that in the struggle for existence his chance of a long life will be much superior to that of the native chiefs; yet from all these admissions, there does not follow the conclusion that, after a limited or unlimited number of generations, the inhabitants of the island will be white.... Our white's qualities would certainly tend very much to preserve him to a good old age, and yet he would not suffice in any number of generations to turn his subjects' descendants white. It may be said that the white colour is not the cause of the superiority. True, but it may be used simply to bring before the senses the way in which qualities belonging to one individual in a large number must be gradually obliterated.[21]

It did not occur to either Jenkin or Darwin that the blending of traits itself was contrary to obvious facts, because if it were true, there would be no difference between different individuals of a species, and all would inexorably proceed towards a monotonous uniformity.

Mendel Discovers the Rules of Heredity

Two years before Jenkin mounted the scathing attack on the theory of evolution, Gregor Mendel, a Moravian monk (Moravia is presently a region in Czech Republic, but it was then a part of the Austrian empire), gave a two part lecture on 8th February and 8th March 1865 at Brünn Natural History Society on the cross-pollinating experiments which he had conducted in his garden for seven years between 1856 and 1863.[22] Mendel selected seven traits in pea plants for cross-pollination experiment: seed shape, seed colour, flower colour, flower position, pod shape, pod colour and stem length. Each character manifested in two different forms, for example, round and wrinkled seeds, white and purple flowers etc. Pea plants could also easily be protected from the influence of foreign pollens, which was vital for the accuracy of result.

The hybrids obtained from cross-pollination in all seven crosses showed interesting results: They were identical to one of their parents. The hybrids from plants of round and wrinkled seeds produced round seeds; the hybrids of white and purple flowers produced purple flowers only. The traits which were transmitted wholly from parents to offspring were called dominant traits by Mendel and the traits which were suppressed were called recessive traits. In the first generation of hybrid plants obtained by self-pollination, among each of the four plants, the recessive character reappeared in one. When the experiment was repeated with seed-bearer plants serving as pollen plants and vice versa, the same results were obtained. It did not matter whether the dominant trait belonged to the seed plant or the pollen plant. This was possible only if the offspring inherited traits from their parents in pairs and they were not blended but existed in the offspring in discrete form (what we now call gene). The purple hybrid plant had both traits purple (P) and white (W) inherited from parents, but because P was the dominant trait, the offspring had purple flowers. In the first generation of hybrid plant, there were four distinct ways in which traits could combine: PP, PW, WP and WW. In first three cases, the offspring would display dominant trait of purple, but in the last case, the offspring would have white flowers. Mendel further cross-pollinated plants differing in two traits, for example, round and yellow seeds with wrinkled and green seeds. The results of the experiment showed that one type of trait (seed shape) was inherited by the offspring independent of the other type of trait (seed colour).

The Brünn Society published Mendel's paper in 1866 in its official *Proceedings*, however, the significance of his experiments was not fully grasped and he faded into near oblivion until three biologists - Hugo de Vries of Holland, Carl Correns of Germany and Erich von Tschermark-Seysenegg of Austria - rediscovered his work almost simultaneously in 1900. Unbeknown to what had happened in faraway Brünn, Jenkin made blending inheritance the lynchpin of his arguments against the theory of evolution, and a rattled Darwin not only conceded his arguments but also proposed the hypothesis of pangenesis, building upon Lamarck's theory of inheritance of acquired characteristics, to tide over the difficulty posed by blending inheritance:

> It is almost universally admitted that cells, or the units of the body, propagate themselves by self-division or proliferation, retaining the same nature, and ultimately becoming converted into the various tissues and substances of the body.... [They] throw off minute granules or atoms, which circulate freely throughout the system, and when supplied with proper nutriment multiply by self-division, subsequently becoming developed into cells like those from which they were derived. These granules for the sake of distinctness may be called cell-gemmules, or, as the cellular theory is not fully established, simply gemmules. They are supposed to be transmitted from the parents to the offspring, and are generally developed in the generation which immediately succeeds, but are often transmitted in a dormant state during many generations and are then developed.... Gemmules are supposed to be thrown off by every cell or unit, not only during the adult state, but during all the stages of development. Lastly, I assume that the gemmules in their dormant state have a mutual affinity for each other, leading to their aggregation either into buds or into the sexual elements. Hence, speaking strictly, it is not the reproductive elements, nor the buds, which generate new organisms, but the cells themselves throughout the body. These assumptions constitute the provisional hypothesis which I have called Pangenesis.[23]

Darwin's emphasis that gemmules were emitted during all stages of life was calculated to provide a mechanism for the inheritance of traits acquired by adaptation to support evolution, but he candidly admitted the tentativeness of his premise: "I am aware that my view is merely a provisional hypothesis or speculation; but until a better one be advanced, it may be serviceable by bringing together a multitude of facts which are at present left disconnected by any efficient cause."[24] But no experimental confirmation of pangenesis was forthcoming; on the contrary, evidence was mounting that reproductive cells alone carried hereditary material and other types of cells had no role to play in transmission of inheritance. Mendel's theory of inheritance would certainly have helped Darwin put a robust defence to Jenkin, but the theory of natural selection would still have remained vulnerable to questioning because it required a mechanism of transmission of acquired traits to offspring, which even Mendel did not offer. As the 19th century drew to close there was little doubt about the fact of evolution, but natural selection as the mechanism of evolution wilted under twin assaults – the insufficiency of the age of the earth and the absence of a mode of transmission of acquired traits.

Modern Synthesis Reconciles Darwinism with Genetics

The first half of the twentieth century witnessed a great stride in the field of genetics, beginning with the rediscovery of Mendel's work, and although Mendelians were initially opposed to natural selection, the outstanding work of Ronald Fisher, JBS Haldane and Sewall Wright ultimately led to the Modern Synthesis – a fusing together of ideas of different branches of biology to explain evolution. The Modern Synthesis altogether jettisoned Darwin's idea that beneficial traits acquired during the lifetime of an individual of a species were passed on to its offspring, instead it argued that evolution took place by a random process of genetic mutation, which produced variation in traits, and on which the natural selection operated. To understand this, we have to first know a bit about genes.

Now we know that the nucleus of cells contains chromosomes and each chromosome consists of protein and a single macromolecule of deoxyribonucleic acid (DNA). The DNA molecule is made up of several nucleotides, which can be likened to small links of a long chain. A gene is a portion of the DNA molecule which carries coded information for the transmission of traits and behaviour from parents to offspring. In the case of asexual reproduction, a cell simply divides into two, which is called mitosis. The chromosomes replicate themselves and then the original and the copy are segregated. Meiosis is a process of creation of gametes (sperm and egg cell). A cell undergoes division twice for creating four gametes, each containing half the number of chromosomes. For example, a normal human cell has 23 pairs of chromosomes – in each pair one chromosome comes from the father and the other from the mother. In the first phase of meiosis, chromosomes replicate themselves thus producing 46 pairs, and then four cells each containing 23 chromosomes are formed. Both sperm and egg cell contain only 23 chromosomes so that when they combine to produce a zygote, it has 23 pairs. Copying errors during replication of DNA as well as exposure to chemicals or radiation can cause mutation of genes.

Natural selection operates on genetic diversity, as the traits that help an individual of a species in survival and reproduction are favoured. Individuals possessing the favourable traits are able to spread their genes faster and others lose the race of life and become extinct. Three conditions are essential for natural selection to work: existence of traits that are favourable in the struggle for existence (for example, a suitable camouflage to deceive predators), inheritability of traits and differential reproduction rate. They should be able to produce more offspring over their lifetime than other individuals. Natural selection does not create a species; rather it acts on existing variety to choose the most suitable for the propagation of life, and herein lies the fundamental difference between Darwin's natural selection and the Modern Synthesis. New genes are truly produced by mutation, a random process, which is happening all the time, but most mutations are neutral. They do not confer any specific advantage to the individual. Some may indeed be harmful, but occasionally a favourable trait does appear. Mutation does not happen in order to be selected; in other words there is no design behind it.

In the modern synthesis, natural selection is not the only process of evolution. There are others: genetic drift and gene flow. Genetic drift occurs in a population of small size. Imagine a hypothetical gene which is responsible for the colour of eyes, which can be either brown or black. It is possible that in a small group of interbreeding population one type of eye colour is eliminated completely over a few generations by chance. It is like getting a series of heads when we toss a coin repeatedly, the probability of getting which is low but not zero. Genetic drift can also occur due to a disaster in which one type of gene is substantially or completely destroyed. Gene flow, on the other hand, is caused by movement of individuals from one group of population to another, introducing genetic variation. Wind and other natural forces can also disperse plant seeds and pollen leading to cross-pollination.

How Did the First Life Arise on the Earth

The discovery of cyanobacteria fossils revealed that life on the earth has existed for more than 3.5 billion years. If mindboggling variety and complexity of life today is the result of a slow process of evolution over 3.5 billion years from the simplest form of life, how did single-celled organisms emerge on the earth? Aleksandr Oparin, a Soviet biochemist, and JBS Haldane – we have discussed him earlier – had independently advanced what is now called Oparin-

Haldane hypothesis in 1920s. They suggested that the primordial earth's atmosphere was rich in methane, ammonia, water vapour and hydrogen with traces of hydrogen sulphide. The mixture was subjected to several energy sources such as lightening, solar radiation and radioactive heat emerging from the crust of earth, which created organic compounds, the building blocks of life. Stanley Miller and Harold Urey, both American chemists, proceeded to test the hypothesis experimentally in 1953, the same year in which Watson and Crick discovered DNA structure. They passed high voltage electric discharge - to mimic natural lightening - through a mixture of ammonia, water vapour, methane and hydrogen, which were thought to be present on the primordial earth. The experiment yielded amino acids, building blocks of protein, confirming the hypothesis, but it gradually went out of favour when evidence surfaced that the atmosphere existing on primordial earth might actually be different from what had been assumed by Miller-Urey. Several variations of the experiment have been attempted since then with different mixture of gases and energy sources: electric discharge, ultraviolet light, electron irradiation, proton irradiation and heat, but scientists have been unable to reach a consensus.

Nucleic acids (DNA and RNA) and protein are basic chemical constituents of life. While nucleic acids are long chains of nucleotides, protein is a long chain of amino acids. A single nucleotide is made up of three components: a nitrogen-containing base - there are five types of bases, namely, adenine (A), cytosine (C), guanine (G), thymine (T) and uracil (U) - a five-carbon sugar molecule either ribose or 2-deoxiribose, and a phosphate group. There are 20 types of amino acids, which combine differently to form thousands of varieties of proteins. For example, red blood cells contain a protein called haemoglobin which carries oxygen to various parts of our bodies. Similarly our eyes contain proteins which are capable of detecting light.

Although Swiss chemist Friedrich Miescher isolated nucleic acid from white blood cells way back in 1869, the structure of DNA was discovered by American biologist James Watson and English physicist Francis Crick in 1953. Imagine a long ladder whose sides are not straight but helical in shape. The sides are made up of sugar-phosphate and each rung a pair of bases. T pairs with A and C pairs with G. Therefore, if one strand of DNA has code ... ACCGTAT ... the other strand will have the code ... TGGCATA ... The two strands of double helix automatically separate during the process of cell division and thereafter each half recreates its complimentary half to complete the process of replication. Thus DNA is passed on from cell to cell and from parents to offspring.

DNA remains confined to the nucleus of a cell whereas protein is made by ribosomes - protein factories - in cytoplasm outside the nucleus. Therefore, the synthesis of protein does not take place directly from DNA. The genetic information contained in base sequence of DNA is copied to RNA, which is also a chain of nucleotides, but it has a single strand. The single-stranded RNA is also made up of sugar-phosphate, but its sugar is a bit different from DNA's sugar. It also contains four bases: A, C, G, but U in place of T. During transcription from DNA to RNA, T base is replaced by U base, and therefore a hypothetical DNA sequence AATGCTTAG becomes AAUGCUUAG after transcription. We know that the entire sequence of DNA does not carry genetic information, therefore, only the portion of DNA containing genes is copied. Thereafter, the RNA strip leaves the nucleus of the cell and heads to a ribosome where the RNA code is deciphered.

There are only four bases but twenty different amino acids. How does a ribosome know which amino acid has to be produced by reading the RNA code? A triplet of nucleotides called codon can be combined in $4 \times 4 \times 4 = 64$ different ways. Each such triplet corresponds to an amino acid; for example, when a ribosome reads AAG amino acid 'lycine' is produced. Since there are 64 possible codons and only 20 amino acids, more than one codon specify the same amino acid. The RNA strip is sequentially deciphered and amino acids are linked together in a growing three dimensional chain to form protein. Start codon tells the ribosome to begin the operation of producing protein and stop codon ceases it. Our bodies have grown with complex organs at right locations to carry out specific functions through this process of DNA decoding and protein synthesis. Therefore, it would not be an exaggeration to say that the mystery of our being is hidden in long sequences of four letters: A, C, G and T.

The synthesis of protein required DNA and RNA; DNA replication as well as RNA transcription needed a number of enzymes to catalyse the reactions, but all enzymes were found to be proteins. Protein could not be made without DNA and RNA, which, in turn, could not be synthesised without protein. Therefore, scientists were caught in the classical chicken-egg paradox – which came first: DNA, RNA or protein?

Francis Crick, Leslie Orgel and Carl Woese in late 1960s outlined 'RNA world' hypothesis, which suggested that RNA performed dual functions of self-replication and growth before the advent of DNA. The belief in RNA world was strengthened when RNA based enzyme 'ribozymes' was discovered in early 1980s, but the critics of the hypothesis consider RNA molecules to be too complex to be created on their own, as well as inherently unstable. In all fairness, the proponents of RNA world never claim that RNA based life was first to emerge on the earth. Similarly, some scientists believe in protein first hypothesis while some others favour co-evolution of protein and nucleic acid simultaneously. Although there is no experimental confirmation of any of the hypotheses, RNA world is generally accepted as the most plausible hypothesis today, which brings us to the final puzzle in explaining the origin of life: how was the first organic polymer - whether DNA, RNA or protein - was created from inorganic molecules.

According to another hypothesis, life was brought on earth from space by comets and asteroids. But if life arrived from elsewhere in the universe to the earth, how did life emerge there? The laws of physics and chemistry are the same everywhere in the universe, and therefore no matter where life arose, the process of creation of life must be similar, if not the same. Despite the best attempt of scientists the origin of life on the earth remains an open question. Nick Lane, a British biochemist and writer, illustrates the prevailing confusion over the origin of life rather accurately:

> This terrain is the playground of retired Nobel laureates and other towering figures in biology; yet for all their learning and intellect, they cannot begin to agree among themselves. Forty years ago, at the dawn of molecular biology, the French biologist Jacques Monad wrote his famous book *Chance and Necessity*, which argues bleakly that the origin of life on earth was a freak accident, and that we are alone in an empty universe.... Since then others have argued the opposite: that life is an inevitable outcome of cosmic chemistry. It will arise quickly, almost everywhere.[25]

If life arose due to a fortuitous combination of existing molecules on the earth in a random stroke, that one rare event might have occurred after billions of other random combinations had failed. Conversely, if life emerged through a slow process of 'chemical evolution', in which simpler molecules acquired the ability to replicate and evolve, it might have taken a very long time to create the first cellular life. Neither can billions of random possibilities be simulated in a laboratory nor do we have the luxury of experimenting over cosmic scale of time. Therefore, the possibility of creating artificial life from matter appears to be extremely dim. And, as long as that remains, the exact process of emergence of life would continue to be shrouded in mystery.

Not so long ago, mankind believed that life was a special creation of God. The variety and complexity of life rendered any other idea counter-intuitive. Since then we have discovered amazing facts, unravelled many layers of ignorance, developed new theories, and yet we have not been able to grasp life in its fullness. We know so much more than our ancestors, and yet a serious doubt lingers in our mind that the secret of life may perhaps never be known.

Hypotheses of Ageing and Consequences of Longevity

We shall now turn to the collective desire of human beings for immortality – or at least longevity. The average life expectancy, which was stagnating near 27 years in 1800, increased marginally to 30 years in 1900, and then more than doubled to 65 years in 2000[26]. As per World Health Organisation's report, the life expectancy at birth has climbed to 71 years in 2013. Jeanne Calment, a French woman, lived for 122 years and holds the record of longest living person to date. The initial spurt in longevity was powered by a sharp reduction in mortality due to control of communicable diseases, beginning with the discovery of smallpox vaccine by the British physician Edward Jenner in 1796. Antibiotics further helped in treating a host of diseases caused by bacteria. Improved hygiene, better nutrition and rapid advancement in medical science have ensured that today we expect to live longer than any time in the history of mankind, and the long held desire of mankind to live forever is now in the realm of serious science rather than alchemy and soothsaying.

The key to long life lies in understanding the process of aging because then it will not be difficult to reverse it. Clive McCay, Mary Crowell and LA Maynard conducted an experiment on white rats – the results of which were published in 1935 – in which one group of rats were given diet containing adequate protein, minerals and vitamins, but restricted in calories, while the other group were fed as many calories as desired by them. It was observed that the rats on restrictive calorie diet survived longer than the other group. McCay's experiment became the basis for calorie restriction hypothesis, which has since been repeated on other animals, including rhesus monkeys, with similar results. Although the underlying mechanism by which life is prolonged remains unclear, it is one of the key areas of research being pursued by scientists to increase longevity in human beings. Low calorie diet of people of Okinawa, an island in Japan, and their long life seem to bolster the belief in calorie restriction hypothesis. However, there is no conclusive evidence of its impact on humans as yet and some scientists even warn of long term potential damage to health.

Oxygen is used by our bodies to convert food into energy, without which we cannot perform daily functions, but it also produces free radicals. Free radicals are highly reactive as they contain unpaired electrons. Hydroxyl radical, for example, is a combination of one atom of oxygen and one atom of hydrogen. Free radicals inflict damage on various macromolecules present in the cells, namely, proteins, lipids and nucleic acids. Though some damage caused to the cells is repairable, organisms accumulate damages over their life time, which leads to aging and ultimately death. This is known as free radical hypothesis of aging, which was proposed by Denham Harman, an American scientist in 1956. If the hypothesis is true, antioxidants like vitamin A, C and E should be able to destroy free radicals and thereby enhance life span. However, the evidence so far has not been definitive and scientists are still arguing about the efficacy of antioxidants in slowing the aging process.

French surgeon Alexis Carrel had demonstrated in the 1920s that a cell could divide and replicate endlessly in proper culture, and this remained the dominant view until 1961 when it was challenged by American cell biologist, Leonard Hayflick. He obtained strains of human cells from aborted foetuses and cultivated them in suitable culture. He was surprised to observe that the older cell strains were replicating slowly compared to the younger cell strains, and eventually they ceased dividing altogether. Hayflick concluded that cells had finite capacity to divide and they died after reaching that limit, now known as Hayflick limit, which are 40 to 60 divisions for human cells. Subsequent research has shown that chromosomes have telomeres - protective regions - at both ends, which are nothing but repetitive sequences of nucleotides. Human telomeres contain 2500 repetitions of sequence TTAGGG. With every cell division telomeres get shortened until a critical limit is reached, after which the cell stops dividing and dies. The special sequence of nucleotides does not code for any protein, therefore, nothing is lost due to shortening of telomeres; rather it prevents loss of genetic information during cell division. It appears as if telomeres act like an inbuilt biological clock that signals cells not to divide and essentially commit suicide.

Hayflick claimed that maximum life span of a species was linked to number of divisions its cells were capable of undergoing: maximum life span of human beings is 110 years (40-60 divisions) and that of Galapagos tortoise is 175 years (90-125 divisions). However, it turned out to be a rather simplistic depiction of a very complex process. Some cells in our brains do not divide at all and last for the entire lifetime whereas some cells have their telomeres repeatedly extended by an enzyme telomerase. Hope was raised that the enzyme could help cells to replicate beyond Hayflick limit, but it was soon found that this was fraught with danger as cancer cells also contained telomerase.

There are many more hypotheses vying with one another to explain aging, but scientists are yet to reach any definitive conclusion. It is plausible that it may be caused by complex interplay of several factors; therefore, our effort to pin it down on a single determinant has failed. Undeterred by these challenges, scientists are pretty confident that human life span can be extended at least up to 200 years in the near future. Google launched California Life Company, Calico, in September 2013 to support life extension research. Aubrey de Grey, a scientist on the forefront of such research, who works in SENS Foundation, believes that humans will live for 1,000 years very soon.

But what would it be like if science were to find a recipe for immortality? Our present population and consumption patterns have severely compromised the ability of earth to sustain human life. The population of the world would increase manifold if human beings were to live for a thousand years, which would inevitably lead to ruthless competition for scarce resources. To control explosive growth of population, birth rate would require to be severely curtailed by allowing very few couples to produce children. And if we were to live forever, there would have to be complete restriction on birth. The world would then become a cesspool of stagnant life, devoid of rejuvenation and freshness, and the process of evolution would come to a grinding halt. If the benefit of immortality, on the other hand, were to be bestowed upon only a selected few, either because of affordability or deliberate policy to check growth, the moral consequences of such a hideous inequality would be beyond our imagination.

Science has not fully explained the origin of life on earth; it is still searching for the missing links in the evolution of human beings from unicellular organism; it has failed to rescue mankind from suffering caused by simple chronic diseases like acidity, migraine etc.; and despite tremendous advancement, the process of aging still remains unclear. Moreover, it is not known, how a living organism loses consciousness at the time of death when all the cells in the body remain alive at the moment. The atoms and the molecules that constitute the body continue to exist and yet the organism becomes lifeless. Granted that human life span has more than doubled in the last two centuries, but it has been accompanied by old age diseases, so much so that societies are contemplating euthanasia to end the terrible suffering a person endures. Therefore, for scientists to claim that they will soon find the elixir of immortality is wishful thinking, as enchanting and as ludicrous as that of yesteryears' soothsayers.

Curse of Immortality

Mahabharata, the great epic has valuable lessons on death and immortality. In the battlefield of Kurukshetra, 11 akshauhinis army of the Kauravas were arrayed against 7 akshauhinis of the Pandavas - one akshauhini comprised of 21,870 chariots, 21,870 elephants, 65,610 cavalry and 1,09,350 infantry. The Kauravas were led by the venerable Bhishma while Dhrishtadyumna was the commander-in-chief of the Pandavas. Earlier, all efforts to settle the territorial dispute peacefully between the two brothers had failed. The two sides blew conch shells, bugles and beat cymbals and drums to signal the beginning of the war. Arjuna asked Lord Krishna to take the chariot in the middle of the field so that he could look upon the warriors with whom he had to fight. He carefully observed the enemy phalanx and he found teachers, relatives and friends facing him. His heart was filled with horror; his hands started trembling, unable to hold the bow firmly; and thus troubled he spoke:

> I do not see how any good can come from killing my own kinsmen in this battle, nor can I, my dear Krishna, desire any subsequent victory, kingdom or happiness. O Govinda, of what avail to us are a kingdom, happiness or life itself when all those for whom we may desire them are now arrayed on

> this battlefield? O Madhusudana, when teachers, fathers, sons, grandfathers, maternal uncles, fathers-in-law, grandsons, brothers-in-law and other relatives are ready to give up their lives and properties and are standing before me, why should I wish to kill them, even though they might otherwise kill me? O maintainer of all living entities, I am not prepared to fight with them even in exchange of the three worlds, let alone this earth. What pleasure will we derive from killing the sons of Dhritarashtra ... O Janardana, although these men, their hearts overtaken by greed, see no fault in killing one's family or quarrelling with friends, why should we, who can see the crime in destroying a family, engage in these acts of sin?[27]

Overwhelmed by grief and compassion, Arjuna sat down on the chariot keeping the bow and arrows aside and refused to fight. Krishna chastised him for allowing weakness to sway his mind at a critical moment and reminded of his duty to fight the war befitting his reputation. Krishna then went on to explain the real nature of existence.

> Never was there a time when I did not exist, nor you, nor all these kings; nor in the future shall any of us cease to be. As the embodied soul continuously passes, in this body, from boyhood to youth to old age, the soul similarly passes into another body at death. A sober person is not bewildered by such a change.... As a person puts on new garments, giving up old ones, the soul similarly accepts new material bodies, giving up the old and useless ones.... One who has taken his birth is sure to die, and after death one is sure to take birth again. Therefore, in the unavoidable discharge of your duty, you should not lament.[28]

He further elaborated:

> That which pervades the entire body you should know to be indestructible. No one is able to destroy that imperishable soul.... For the soul there is neither birth nor death at any time. He has not come into being, does not come into being,

> and will not come into being. He is unborn, eternal, ever-existing and primeval. He is not slain when the body is slain.[29]

Dharma (duty) and *karma* (deed) are the core tenets of Hinduism; when one deviates from *dharma* one earns bad *karmas* and conversely good *karmas* are gained by adhering to *dharma*. At the time of death, the soul of a person leaves to acquire a new body, not necessarily of a human being, but any of 8.4 million species in the world (coincidently the current estimate of number of species on the earth is 8.7 million), which is determined by the balance of *karmas* of the person accumulated over the life time and his craving for the fulfilment of unfulfilled desires. Although animals and plants also have soul, they do not earn good or bad *karmas* as they do not possess free will to act. Their behaviour is caused by natural instincts - a lion kills a deer only to satisfy its hunger. A human being takes birth as a different species to expiate for bad *karmas* performed during his life, and when accumulated bad *karmas* are exhausted he is reborn as a human being; thus the cycle of birth and death continues ceaselessly until the soul is liberated (*moksha*) and unites with *brahman*, which is the highest attainment in Hindu thought.

Austrian physicist, Erwin Schrodinger, best known for his contribution to quantum mechanics, was hugely interested in the nature and origin of life, but he approached towards it through physics, and at the end of his quest, he concluded:

> From the early great Upanishads the recognition ATMAN = BRAHMAN (the personal self equals the omnipresent, all-comprehending eternal self) was in Indian thought considered, far from being blasphemous, to represent the quintessence of deepest insight into the happenings of the world. The striving of all the scholars of *Vedanta* was, after having learnt to pronounce with their lips, really to assimilate in their minds this grandest of all thoughts. Again,

> the mystics of many centuries, independently, yet in perfect harmony with each other (somewhat like the particles in an ideal gas) have described, each of them, the unique experience of his or her life in terms that can be condensed in the phrase: DEUS FACTUS SUM (I have become God).[30]

Brahman - the universal consciousness - is the supreme, indivisible and eternal reality pervading the entire cosmos. The perception that soul - *atman* - is separate from *brahman* is created by *maya*. The cessation of this duality is *moksha*, when one sees oneself in the whole universe and the whole universe in oneself.

Indian philosophy - which includes Buddhism and Jainism - takes a cyclic view of life. Life cannot exist without death and death without life. Birth and death are not two discrete events but are a part of cosmic continuum. "In some obscure way we realize that life and death are but two phases - antagonistic but complimentary - of a single reality. Creation and destruction become one in the act of love, and during a fraction of a second man has a glimpse of a more perfect state of being."[31] It is, therefore, not surprising that *yogis* and *sanyasis* describe their departure from the world as merely abandonment of body, a temporary place for the resting of soul. It is not something to be grieved over, but a natural progression of the cosmic cycle. There are several examples of people deciding to leave the body voluntarily by refusing to eat; Hindus call it *prayopavesa* and Jains *santhara*. It, however should not be confused with suicide as the impulse for bringing closure to life is not frustration and despair, rather it is a sense of fulfilment, a feeling that one's purpose of staying has been achieved and it is time to move on. It is a gradual, non-violent process of abandonment of body as opposed to suicide which is a sudden violent strike on the body.

As the sun set on the eighteenth day of the *Mahabharata* war, the 11 *akshauhinis* army of the Kauravas lay completely annihilated, with only four warriors surviving - Duryodhana, Ashwatthama, Kritavarman and Kripacharya. Thereafter, Duryodhana was also mortally wounded, and later died, in a club duel with Bhima. An eerie silence engulfed the battlefield, which was only broken by the howls of animals, making the night even more dreadful. The dead bodies and disfigured limbs of soldiers were strewn all around reminding the victors of the futility of war and fuelling the ember of revenge in the vanquished. Tormented by humiliating defeat, Ashwatthama was restless and unable to sleep when he observed an owl attacking crows that were sleeping on a tree. The attack was so sudden and fierce that the crows did not have any time to react. Ashwatthama conceived a plan to kill the Pandavas in the middle of the night while they were sleeping in their tent. He immediately woke up Kritavarman and Kripacharya and disclosed his intention. They were taken aback as it was totally against the established canons of war and tried to reason with Ashwatthama, but he was possessed by an intense desire to avenge the death of Duryodhana. Finally, Kritavarman and Kripacharya acquiesced in the ghastly act of cowardice, but their plan went awry and they ended up killing the Pandavas' sons instead. When Pandavas learnt of the death of their innocent children, they were furious and wanted to kill Ashwatthama at once, but Lord Krishna adjudged that death would not redeem his sin and cursed him to live for three thousand years.

Thirty six years later, Lord Krishna was accidently killed by a hunter's arrow while he was resting on a river bank. Parikshit was anointed the king of Hastinapur and the Pandavas along with Draupadi started their journey for the heavens, but one by one four brothers as well as Draupadi died on the way and only Yudhishthir could reach there. By then all the dramatis personae of *Mahabharata* had departed except Ashwatthama. The galaxies were moving further apart; the earth was going round the sun; the tides were turning, rivers flowing; time was moving past, only Ashwatthama remained stuck. His body weakened but never gave up and the mind accumulated the burden of time. He repented, sought forgiveness, but there was none to forgive him; he wanted to escape the dreadful memory, but there was nothing familiar to distract him; he wanted liberation, but he was instead condemned to the ordeal of immortality.

Nothing is ever created and nothing is ever destroyed – this is the fundamental principle of the universe. Energy may change its form; light energy can be converted into electrical energy; kinetic energy of waterfall is used to drive turbines which produce electrical energy. In any chemical reaction mass is conserved although atoms change places. Albert Einstein established equivalence between mass and energy, bringing unity between two entirely different parameters. The transmigration of soul, therefore, can be said to be philosophical extension of the same fundamental principle so abundantly observed in the universe in respect of such physical parameters as mass, energy and charge.

Science has unravelled many mysteries of life but the understanding of consciousness and death continues to elude it, yet it dreams of conquering death, which indeed may not even be desirable, for immortality, besides its moral consequences, can trap life in a fate worse than death. The hypothesis of transmigration of souls may be false; may be nothing happens after death; consciousness may have no existence outside the material body; but it is comforting to believe that one will continue to exist in the universe, even though in a different form.

Notes and References

1. *Asking about Life* by Allan J Tobin and Jennie Dusheck, p 376, Third edition, Brooks/Cole, Belmont, USA, 2005.
2. As quoted *ibid*, p 376.

3. *Ibid*, p 377.
4. *What is Life?: Investigating the Nature of Life in the Age of Synthetic Biology* by Edward Regis, p 90, OUP, New York 2009.
5. *Ibid*, pp 90-1.
6. *The Process of Science* by Anthony Carpi and Anne E Egger, p 107, Visionlearning, New Canaan, USA, 2011.
7. *The Private Science of Louis Pasteur* by Gerald L Geison, p 120, Princeton University Press, New Jersey, 1995.
8. As quoted in *The Greatest Show on Earth: The Evidence for Evolution* by Richard Dawkins, p 418, Free Press, New York, 2009.
9. *Micrographia or Some Physiological Descriptions of Minute Bodies* by Robert Hooke, pp 113-4, Cosimo Classics, New York, 2007.
10. *A History of the Life Sciences* by Lois N Magner, p 138, Third edition, Marcel Dekker, Inc, New York, 2002.
11. "An Abstract of a Letter from Mr Anthony Leewenhoeck", *Philosophical Transactions* of the Royal Society of London, Vol 14, No 159, 1684, p 568.
12. *Microscopical Researches into the Accordance in the Structure and Growth of Animals and Plants* by Theodor Schwann, pp 191-2, the Sydenham Society, London, 1847.
13. *Ibid*, p 39.
14. *A History of the Life Sciences* by Lois N Magner, p 185, Third edition, Marcel Dekker, Inc, New York, 2002.
15. *Principles of Cell Biology* by George Plopper, p 49, Second edition, Jones & Bartlett Learning, USA, 2016.
16. *Charles Darwin: The Man and His Influence* by Peter J Bowler, pp 111-2, Cambridge University Press, 1996.
17. *The Origin of Species* by Charles Darwin, p 499, PF Collier & Son, New York, 1909.
18. *Ibid*, pp 528-9.
19. *Ibid*, p 7.
20. "Darwin and the Dilemma of Geological Time", Joe D Burchfield, *Isis*, Vol 65, No 3, 1974, pp 300-21.
21. Review of "The Origin of Species", Fleeming Jenkin, *The North British Review*, Vol 46, No 92, 1867, pp 289-90.
22. *The Monk in the Garden: The Lost and Found Genius of Gregor Mendel, the Father of Genetics* by Robin Henig, p 5, A Mariner Book, New York, 2001.

exclusively on mental characteristics (such as pleasure, happiness or desires) can be particularly restrictive when making interpersonal comparisons of well-being and deprivation," because "it can be easily swayed by mental conditioning and adaptive attitudes."[17]

Doubtless some slaves must have been happy as people reconcile to an unjust social or political order because of mental conditioning and adaptive attitudes, and therefore the utilitarian argument can become a justification for the perpetuation of an unjust and oppressive order, or at least dissuade people from fighting for a radical change in the system. Sen, therefore, argued that there were certain rights and freedoms that were inalienable and should be available to all. These rights and freedoms have intrinsic worth irrespective of whether they produce happiness or not. Further, the oft repeated criticism of utilitarianism that it fails to differentiate between different types of happiness - taking perverse delight in the misery of others and getting profound satisfaction in altruistic acts are given equal weight in utilitarianism - is also echoed by Sen. Therefore, he pitched for a broader definition of human well-being:

> There are many fundamentally different ways of seeing the quality of living, and quite a few of them have some immediate plausibility. You could be well off, without being well. You could be well, without being able to lead the life you wanted. You could have got the life you wanted, without being happy. You could be happy, without having much freedom. You could have a good deal of freedom, without achieving much. We can go on.[18]

On this philosophical foundation, Sen developed what is called the 'capability approach' of measuring well-being. He argued that possessions were not important in themselves. It was not important as to what we possessed, but what we were able to do and be with that possession.

Sen called these doings and beings functionings. To live a healthy life, to get proper education, to participate in public affairs, to enjoy religious freedom etc, all these are examples of functioning, which has a very wide connotation. He did not undermine the importance of commodities but asserted that human beings should have capabilities to convert these into achievements (functionings). A car will be of little use to a woman who is not permitted to obtain a license, and thus prevented from driving the car because of which she cannot achieve the functioning of say "working outside the home in a factory or shop or office." A child cannot get proper education if there is no school in his neighbourhood although he might possess requisite books. People are unable to translate commodities into functioning due to lack of freedom and public action. Therefore, higher level of per capita income need not necessarily translate into functioning, which is demonstrated by the fact that "Saudi Arabia is rich but has lower life expectancy than the Indian state of Kerala" and survival chances of African Americans living in Harlem, New York is lower than the citizens of China and Kerala, who have much lower incomes.[19] Therefore, the well-being should be measured, not by per capita income, but by attainment of certain functionings. However, Sen refused to prescribe a definitive list of functionings that could be universally used to measure well-being arguing that any such list should be context specific and decided through a reasoned public debate.

Pakistani economist Mahbub ul Haq developed the Human Development Index (HDI) in 1990 – largely inspired by Sen's capabilities approach of measuring well-being – a more broad-based indicator of human welfare, comprising of per capita income, life expectancy at birth and literacy rate. It was further refined in later years by incorporating income and gender inequality. Since then, HDI is published every year by the United Nations Development Programme and widely used all over the world for reorienting policies to achieve development and well-being. The selection of three indicators of HDI, as also their weights, can always be debated – Sen himself described the process of selection as an act of reasoning – but the capability approach faces a more fundamental constraint.

Average life expectancy at birth, one of the three components of HDI, is a measure of a functioning, namely, living a sufficiently long and healthy life, but the question is how accurately it measures what it intends to measure. A person X lives for 80 years, of which 48 years is disease free; another person Y lives for 60 years, of which 48 years is disease free. Who has lived a long and healthy life, X or Y? In terms of absolute number of healthy years, both score equally, but in percentage terms Y's score is better. What if both score equally in percentage terms, but total life span of X is greater than Y. A total life span of 80 years with 70% healthy years may be preferable over a total life span of 50 years with same percent of healthy years but beyond a certain point the fear of increased physical suffering may cast its shadow over the desire for longer life. If I propose that people may live for 150 years, of which 105 years would be healthy and remaining 45 years would be spent fighting various diseases, I do not know how many people would accept it. More interestingly, if a choice is given between living for 80 years with 80% healthy years and 60 years with 100% healthy years, the temptation of living the entire life without any suffering may compensate for the loss of a few years of life.

We have taken into consideration thus far only the period of illness and not its intensity assuming that one type of illness is equivalent to other type irrespective of debilitation it causes and suffering it entails; but in reality, suffering from cancer and slow but chronic pain due to migraine for the same amount of time cannot be equated. The degree of debilitation and suffering caused by illnesses varies widelv and it must be accounted for if an accurate measure of 'healthy life' has to be evolved. That would mean assigning weights to different diseases. Further, the distribution of the period of illness over the full life span is no less important. It can be argued that any debilitation during early years can impair the capability of a person considerably, if not irreversibly, therefore preventing him from becoming what he wants to become and doing what he wants to do. Equally vehemently the opposite can be argued too that a similar illness during the prime of youth will lead to complete loss of productive years. Let us assume a hypothetical situation in which it is known that a person has to suffer from six bouts of serious illness during his entire lifetime. But he has the choice to distribute the periods of illness according to his will. Is there an objective way of doing this or will the response vary from person to person? There will be an element of subjectivity in the choice. In fact, the distribution of periods of illness over entire life time is even more contentious than assigning weights to different illnesses on the basis of their intensity.

The point that I am trying to make is that a seemingly simple task of finding an accurate measure of functioning 'healthy life' gets entangled in a web of complexity; what appears so commonsensical, at first, turns out to be much more complicated than expected. Life expectancy is an objective measure of 'healthy life', but it is not precise. A precise measure can be developed by taking into account complex issues such as discussed above, but complexity, while improving the accuracy of measurement, brings an element of judgement, and hence subjectivity - the very thing Sen wanted to avoid.

It has been assumed so far that the selection of functioning(s) is an entirely objective exercise, but it is a task that cannot be taken up completely outside the confines of the social, political and cultural milieu, and in that sense Sen's prescription of choosing a set of functionings (even through a reasoned public debate) cannot remain completely uncontaminated from mental conditioning caused by the context. While prescribing an authoritative list of functionings disregards the socio-cultural context and sounds paternalistic, relying on it raises the same problem to avoid which he abandoned equating well-being with psychological happiness.

Sen's emphasis on objective well-being is understandable – although we have seen that both the selection of functioning and finding its precise measure are not entirely free from the prejudice and bias of the person choosing it – but undermining psychological happiness is fraught with danger. Certainly, we would not want a society in which all material comforts are available; in which social, political and economic institutions are just and fair; but people are unhappy; and depression and suicide rates are high. Therefore, psychological happiness is as important, if not more, as objective well-being, a subject to which we shall turn our attention.

Measuring Subjective Well-being

The research on subjective well-being (SWB) – which started with a simple survey in which people were asked to select one of the alternatives that best described their state of SWB: very happy, quite happy, not so happy, not at all happy etc – has taken rapid strides, with the method of measuring SWB acquiring more sophistication. Hadley Cantril, who was an American psychologist, pioneered what is known as "Self Anchoring Striving Scale". In Cantril's survey, a person was asked to describe his wishes and hopes, the fulfilment of which would constitute the best possible life for him, and this was given a value of ten. Then he was asked to do exactly the opposite – to tell his fears and worries – the worst possible life he could imagine, which was given a value of zero. Finally, the person was asked which number between zero and ten on this imaginary ladder best described his present situation.

In 1974, Richard Easterlin, a Professor of Economics in the USA, published a seminal paper "Does Economic Growth Improve the Human Lot", in which he analysed the data obtained on self-reported happiness from various surveys conducted in the USA as well as different countries; and he arrived at startling conclusions: Within a country, rich people were generally happier than poor people, but over a period of time happiness did not seem to increase with rising income. Easterlin admitted that time series data were not easily available from different countries, with the exception of the USA, and therefore "one must be cautious about drawing any strong conclusions from the limited United States time series [data] studied here."[20] Further, he could not find any significant correlation between income and happiness in cross-country comparison of the data. Easterlin's conclusions were based on the analysis of 17 Gallup-poll type simple surveys and 13 Cantril type surveys conducted across different countries during 1946-70. The findings of the survey came to be known as Easterlin paradox in happiness literature. Easterlin attempted to explain the paradox by arguing that if everybody tried to move up the Cantril's ladder – and indeed moved up – the relative position between any two persons remains unchanged, and hence happiness did not increase. The line of argument was supported by the statements of Indians and Americans in Cantril's survey: The material aspirations of Indians were modest compared to those of Americans, and therefore the 'tens' of Americans on Cantril scale differed substantially from the 'tens' of Indians in absolute material terms.

Easterlin paradox has become a contentious subject in happiness research as also an ideological battleground for those who believe that increasing per capita income – at least beyond a point – does not increase happiness or increases only marginally and those who believe that there is strong correlation between income and happiness. The champions of free market and those who argue for more redistributive policy also use the data to bolster their claim. Since 1974, the data obtained from happiness surveys have multiplied and both groups have relied on latest surveys to buttress their claims. For example, Michael Hagerty and Ruut Veenhoven, both Dutch sociologists, studied the data from 21 countries and concluded that happiness a nd income indeed went together, but the conclusion was not supported by their own evidence which showed strong correlation between income and happiness in only 7 out of 21 countries. Further they did not find any evidence that increased happiness was caused by rising income, ie, no causality could be established between income and happiness. Easterlin hypothesis that happiness depends on relative income and not on absolute income was also tested by Hagerty and Veenhoven but again the evidence was not conclusive either way.[21]

Amidst conflicting studies what can be said with near certainty is that the available evidence does not conclusively prove that higher income causes increased happiness. Researchers have also studied the impact of non-economic variables like health, family life and social, political and economic freedom on happiness, but, there too, no clinching evidence of correlation, let alone causation, has been discovered. In addition to Easterlin's relative income hypothesis, there are two other hypotheses that might explain the paradox. In 1971, Philip Brickman and Donald Campbell, American psychologists, argued that happiness of a person was affected by good or bad events only temporarily, and over a period of time it tended to reach a level that was intrinsic to him.[22] Empirical support for the theory came in a study of lottery winners and paraplegics. It was found that the happiness level of people who won a large sum in lottery and those who did not were identical, and paraplegics were not substantially unhappier than normal people.[23] Neuroscience supports this view, as the brain responds quickly to a novel event and is slow to pick familiar events, which is fundamental for survival.

All of us have experienced this phenomenon of adaptation or habituation: The first air journey is always the most memorable, the next less so and gradually the novelty wears off. One feels as tired after a two hour air journey as one used to feel after a sixteen hour train journey. "Every desirable experience - passionate love, a spiritual high, the pleasure of a new possession, the exhilaration of success - is transitory," writes David Myers[24], another American, psychologist, echoing what Lord Krishna said to Arjuna in *Gita,* "Whatsoever enjoyment is produced out of contact with the outside world is only a source of misery. It has a beginning and an end, therefore a wise man, O son of Kunti, does not revel in it."[6] However, the extent to which adaptation occurs is now a matter of intense debate. The unexpected loss of a child is emotionally so devastating that it permanently alters the happiness set point of a person. There is a growing body of research which indicates that the adaptation is not complete particularly in non-monetary matters such as health, family, friendship etc.

Finally, the aspiration-adjustment hypothesis proclaims that as soon as a goal is achieved we shift the goal post, which means that the distance between aspiration and achievement is never bridged. Therefore a person rarely reports that he is getting happier. Easterlin tested the hypothesis through surveys designed to elicit people aspirations in different stages of life: youth, middle age and so on, and his results confirmed that aspirations tended to rise with achievements.[25] The fabrics of three hypotheses purporting to explain the Easterlin paradox are delicately interwoven in a manner that makes it difficult to disentangle them. An achievement gives temporary happiness because not only do we adapt to the situation gradually but also we see others moving ahead. Adaptation and comparison, in turn, generate new aspirations.

We can never be unhappy about something that does not exist; fantasy can never cause unhappiness. People were not unhappy fifty years back because there was no mobile phone, but today the fact of not being able to afford a mobile phone may cause unhappiness. We are not unhappy that we do not live for 200 years. If an 80 year old person dies, we say he has lived his life fully, but we feel sad if someone dies at 40. To live till 80 years is a possibility – in fact reasonable probability, to live for 200 years a fantasy. Fantasy becomes desire if it acquires a hint of possibility, whose catalyst is comparison – If he has, why can't I? The closer the person the stronger is the tendency for comparison. Easterlin's cross country comparison fails to find any correlation between income and life satisfaction precisely because Indians do not compare themselves with Americans and vice versa. The comparison is always between the comparable.

A 'Remembering Self' and an 'Experiencing Self'

The criticisms of survey method are many: Some obvious – self reported happiness fluctuates widely depending on the mood at the time of reporting. Some less obvious – our responses are influenced by socially desired behaviour; but experts continued to use it as a, and perhaps the only, tool for measuring happiness in the absence of a more reliable method. In 1996 Daniel Kahneman, a Princeton University psychologist conducted a survey of patients undergoing colonoscopy. The patients were divided into two groups: The first group underwent a normal procedure and in the case of second group an additional three minutes were added to the procedure during which the pain was tapered. They were asked to report the intensity of pain every minute during the procedure on a scale of 0 to 10. After the procedure, they were again asked to rate the 'total discomfort' during the procedure. The results indicated that the second group reported entire procedure to be less painful than the first group. The memories of the patients were swayed by the less painful concluding moments of the procedure.[26]

Kahneman argued that every person had two selves: A 'remembering self' and an 'experiencing self' and both recorded the events of life differently. Surveys elicit response from the 'remembering self' and not the 'experiencing self'. He developed a method called Day Reconstruction Method (DRM) in which a participant was asked to narrate in detail how he lived the previous day. The day was then divided into various episodes with time duration and then he was asked to rate each episode on the basis of positive and negative feelings experienced by him. Thus Kahneman tried to measure the happiness recorded by the 'experiencing self'. The results of DRM studies were interesting: "Experienced well-being is on average unaffected by marriage, not because marriage makes no difference to happiness but because it changes some aspects of life for the better and others for the worse."[27] Surprisingly, more educated persons reported higher stress (low experienced well-being) but higher life satisfaction (high remembered well-being). Ill-heath badly affected the experienced well-being but not as much, life satisfaction.[28] Income after a threshold did not improve experienced well-being but had beneficial effect on life satisfaction:

> The satiation level beyond which experienced well-being no longer increases was a household income of about $ 75,000 in high-cost areas (it could be less in areas where the cost of living is lower). The average increase of experienced well-being associated with incomes beyond that level was precisely zero. This is surprising because higher income undoubtedly permits the purchase of many pleasures,

> including vacations in interesting places and opera tickets, as well as an improved living environment. Why do these added pleasures not show up in reports of emotional experience? A plausible interpretation is that higher income is associated with a reduced ability to enjoy the small pleasures of life. There is suggestive evidence in favour of this idea: priming students with the idea of wealth reduces the pleasure their face expresses as they eat a bar of chocolate![29]

Further:

> There is a clear contrast between the effects of income on experienced well-being and on life satisfaction. Higher income brings with it higher satisfaction, well beyond the point at which it ceases to have any positive effect on experience. The general conclusion is as clear for well-being as it was for colonoscopies: people's evaluations of their lives and their actual experience may be related, but they are also different.[30]

Kahneman provided deep insight into the complex phenomenon of happiness, but as far as solving the jigsaw puzzle of happiness is concerned, we are no closer to the solution. Firstly, Kahneman started with the assumption that life satisfaction was a flawed measure of happiness but ended arguing that both experienced well-being and life satisfaction were important elements of happiness. Mahatma Gandhi or Nelson Mandela would not have fought against injustices – spending large parts of the life in jails enduring tremendous suffering (low experienced well-being) – unless they derived immense happiness from the achievement of their goals. In what ratio experienced well-being and life satisfaction influences our overall happiness can only be a matter of speculation as it will vary from person to person.

Secondly, DRM technique cannot fully capture even the experienced well-being of a person because of limited number of samples - after all how many times can a person be subjected to this method. Experience sampling method invented by Mihaly Csikszentmihalyi, a Hungarian psychologist, provides more accurate results in which individuals are prompted by an electronic device at random intervals during the day to report where he is and with whom, what he is doing and his intensity of feelings on a numerical scale. Practical difficulty of obtaining large number of experience samples aside, all self-reported methods face a fundamental problem. Imagine two persons: One uses *yard* and the other *metre* for measuring height. Both of them report that their heights are 1.8. Are they equal in height, clearly not? So when people mark 7 on the happiness scale, are they equally happy or each person uses different unit to measure happiness. The same arguments can be applied to reporting of different feelings like pain, anger, worry, pleasure, calm etc separately.

Further, different feelings, good and bad, can be coalesced into a single parameter only by giving weights to them, but each person will assign a separate set of weights to them. The absence of a standard unit to measure different feelings and the compulsion to assign arbitrary weights to them make the task of measuring experienced well-being highly subjective. Scientists are now searching for biochemical and neurological evidence of happiness. They have identified certain hormones which may be linked with good and bad feelings. Brain imaging has revealed the difference in the response of the brain to a pleasant and an unpleasant feeling. Even if we were to find a set of hormones or brain activity by which the state of momentary happiness could be measured objectively, the subjective happiness felt by two different individuals with same levels of hormones or similar type of brain response could vary.

Perhaps you are not persuaded yet. So let us hypothetically assume a device that continuously measures experienced well-being of a person objectively through biochemical or neurological method. For overall positive feeling at any instant the device reads a positive number proportional to the intensity of the positive feeling and vice versa. The data are collected for a person over his entire life time and the total experienced well-being comes to X units. Is the total experienced well-being more important or the average? Is X units experienced over 40 years equal to X units experienced over 60 years? What about its distribution over time? Is a flatter curve of experienced well-being preferable to one with extreme peaks and troughs or vice versa? In answering these questions, we would again be treading into the subjective domain.

Measure of Unhappiness

What gives happiness can be found only if we know what happiness is, which we do not seem to know despite so much scientific and philosophical inquiry. Is it possible to understand happiness by studying its exact opposite, that is, unhappiness? Depression and suicide are two indicators with which we can quarrel the least, particularly the latter which is unambiguously a manifestation of extreme unhappiness. The data on depression may be hard to compare because of the definitional problem and the likelihood of underestimation of number of depressed people due to lack of mental health professionals and fear of social stigmatisation in some culture. However, the data on suicide rate are more accurately available, and therefore they can be easily compared both within a country and across countries.

Emile Durkheim, who is regarded as the father of sociology, wrote a seminal book on suicide in 1897 in which he studied differing suicide rates among Catholics and Protestants and proposed that suicide rate in a society was inversely proportional to the level of social integration and social regulation. Since then voluminous research has been conducted by the social scientists to understand suicide and the factors causing it. The picture that emerges is very complex, and often contradictory: Suicide rate in rich countries like South Korea, Japan and the USA is high and suicide is completely absent among *Piraha* tribesmen of Amazon, whose life is a daily struggle against various odds; but the incidence of suicide in aboriginal people also widely vary - low in native American tribe of Pomo and high in Kwakiutl tribe; divorce is positively associated with suicide in the USA, but negatively in Australia; African Americans are less likely to commit suicide compared to White Americans.[31]

However, there is a broad agreement that "lack of social integration of individuals as measured by divorce, absence of children, higher female labour force participation, and higher ethno-linguistic heterogeneity raises the suicide rate, whereas a higher marriage rate lowers it."[32] The most contentious issue in suicide research - as was the case in happiness research - is the correlation between income and suicide. Some researchers conclude that income is positively associated with suicide whereas others point out the opposite disregarding the fact that lack of social integration is a characteristic of an economically developed society. Eric Neumayer, a German economist, found that suicide rate was negatively associated with income up to a threshold level of $ 30,700 after which higher income meant higher suicide.[33] In a study of cross-national suicide rates in 72 countries, David Lester, a British-American psychologist, "identified thirteen independent orthogonal factors for the social variables, only one of which was associated with suicide rates. This factor was economic development, with high loadings from such social variables as low population growth and high gross domestic product per capita."[34]

Lester puts forward an idea, which, of course, is very difficult to prove empirically, that when you have "fewer external causes to blame for your misery" your self-worth diminishes and you tend to vent the frustration at yourself. You become the cause of your own failure, which could have been attributed to a variety of external factors like race, caste, economic status, lack of opportunity etc in a more imperfect society.[35] The successful straddles across without any self-doubt or humility, and the failed one cringes in his own failure. How ironic that our effort to improve standard of living, eliminate discrimination and create a better society may end up in producing socially dysfunctional individuals inclined to taking their own lives.

Philosophers have long denied any link between money and happiness, happiness researchers have failed to establish it and suicide research points that extreme form of unhappiness may well increase in the pursuit of money. Whether we employ Sen's capability approach, Cantril's life satisfaction ladder or Kahneman's experienced well-being, happiness remains as elusive as ever. The harder we try to unravel the enigma of happiness, more elusive it becomes. It refuses to be captured in a formula, a mathematical expression however complicated. Perhaps "happiness - as a simple, universal, unitary phenomenon - simply may not be out there in the world for the scientist to find."[36] The existing scientific knowledge and philosophical wisdom can only sharpen our understanding of happiness, but the quest for happiness is - and will remain - an intensely personal quest, the path to which has to be trodden by us in spiritual aloneness. We have to find our own way to reconcile with the multitude, to live in harmony with the other, possibly even with unhappiness.

Notes and References

1. *The Chhandogya Upanishad* by Swami Krishnananda, pp 182-3, The Divine Life Society, India, 2004.
2. *Nicomachean Ethics by Aristotle,* translated by DP Chase, p 13, George Routledge & Sons, 1910.
3. *Happiness and the Art of Being: An Introduction to the Philosophy and*

Practice of the Spiritual Teachings of Bhagvan Sri Ramana by Michael James, p 49, Fourth PDF edition, CreateSpace, 2012.

4. *The Chhandogya Upanishad* by Swami Krishnananda, pp 186-9, The Divine Life Society, India, 2004.
5. *The Chandogyopanishad* by Dr Ganganatha Jha, pp 402-3, Poona Oriental Book Agency, 1942.
6. *The Bhagavad Gita: According to Gandhi*, p 159, Orient Publishing, New Delhi, 2016.
7. "In Search of the Present: Nobel Lecture" by Octavio Paz. https://www.nobelprize.org/nobel_prizes/literature/laureates/1990/paz-lecture.html (accessed on 22nd October 2017)
8. *Happiness and the Art of Being: An Introduction to the Philosophy and Practice of the Spiritual Teachings of Bhagvan Sri Ramana* by Michael James, p 1, Fourth PDF edition, CreateSpace, 2012.
9. *The Philosophy of the Panchdasi* by Swami Krishnananda, p 183, eBook, The Divine Life Society, India. https://www.swami-krishnananda.org/panch/Philosophy_Panchadasi.pdf (accessed on 6th November 2017)
10. *Happiness and the Art of Being: An Introduction to the Philosophy and Practice of the Spiritual Teachings of Bhagvan Sri Ramana* by Michael James, p 60, Fourth PDF edition, CreateSpace, 2012.
11. As quoted in *In the Buddha's Words: An Anthology of Discourses from the Pali Canon*, edited by Bhikkhu Bodhi, pp 281-2, Wisdom Publications, Inc, Somerville, 2005.
12. https://www.jfklibrary.org/Research/Research-Aids/Ready-Reference/RFK-Speeches/Remarks-of-Robert-F-Kennedy-at-the-University-of-Kansas-March-18-1968.aspx (accessed on 22nd October 2017)
13. *An Introduction to the Principles of Morals and Legislation* by Jeremy Bentham, p 2, Oxford Press, 1823.
14. *Ibid*, p 3.
15. *A Fragment on Government* by Jeremy Bentham, p 93, Oxford Press, 1891.
16. *On Ethics and Economics* by Amartya Sen, pp 33-4, Oxford University Press, New Delhi, 1990.
17. *Development as Freedom* by Amartya Sen, p 62, Oxford University Press, 2001.
18. *The Standard of Living, The Tanner Lectures by Amartya Sen et al*, edited by Geoffrey Hawthorn, p 1, Cambridge University Press, 1988.

19. "The Economics of Life and Death", Amartya Sen, *Scientific American*, pp 44-5, May 1993.
20. "Does Economic Growth Improve the Human Lot? Some Empirical Evidence" by Richard Easterlin in *Nations and Households in Economic Growth: Essays in Honor of Moses Abramovitz*, edited by Paul David and Melvin Reder, p 111, Academic Press, Inc, New York, 1974 (Full paper: pp 89-126).
21. "Wealth and Happiness Revisited: Growing National Income Does Go with Greater Happiness", Michael R Hagerty and Ruut Veenhoven, *Social Indicators Research*, Vol 64, No 1, 2003, pp 1-27.
22. "Hedonic Relativism and Planning the Good Society by PD Brickman and DT Campbell", in *Adaptation Level Theory: A Symposium*, edited by MH Appley, pp 287-304, Academic Press, New York, 1972.
23. "Lottery Winners and Accident Victims: Is Happiness Relative?", PD Brickman, D Coates and R Janoff-Bulman, *Journal of Personality and Social Psychology*, Vol 36, No 8, 1978, pp 917-27.
24. *The Pursuit of Happiness: Discovering the Pathway to Fulfilment, Well-Being, and Enduring Personal Joy* by David G Myers, p 53, HarperCollins, New York, 1992.
25. "A Puzzle for Adaptive Theory", Richard Easterlin, *Journal of Economic Behaviour and Organization*, Vol 56, No 4, 2004, pp 513-21.
26. "Memories of Colonoscopy: A Randomized Trial, Donald A Redelmeier", Joel Katz and Daniel Kahneman, *PAIN*, Vol 104, No 1, 2003, pp 187-94.
27. *Thinking, Fast and Slow* by Daniel Kahneman, pp 400-1, Farrar, Straus and Giroux, New York, 2013.
28. *Ibid*, p 396.
29. *Ibid*, p 397.
30. *Ibid*, p 397.
31. "Suicide and Culture", David Lester, *World Cultural Psychiatry Research Review*, Vol 3, No 2, 2008, pp 51-68.
32. "Are Socio-economic Factors Valid Determinants of Suicide? Controlling for National Cultures of Suicide with Fixed-Effects Estimation", Eric Neumayer, *Cross-Cultural Research*, Vol 37, No 3, 2003, pp 322-3.
33. *Ibid*, p 317.
34. "Suicide and Culture", David Lester, *World Cultural Psychiatry Research Review*, Vol 3, No 2, 2008, p 52.

35. http://www.freakonomics.com/2011/06/21/the-suicide-paradox-full-transcript (accessed on 22nd October 2017)

36. "In Pursuit of Happiness Research: Is It Reliable? What Does It Imply for Policy?", Will Wilkinson, *Policy Analysis*, No 590, April 11, 2007, p 12, Cato Institute. https://www.cato.org/publications/policy-analysis/pursuit-happiness-research-is-it-reliable-what-does-it-imply-policy (accessed on 4th November 2017)

4

How Real is Reality?

> Do you really believe that the moon only exists when I am looking at it?
> – *Albert Einstein*

> Observations not only disturb what has to be measured, they produce it.... We compel [the electron] to assume a definite position.... We ourselves produce the results of measurements.
> – *Pascual Jordan*

Greek philosopher Plato in his book *The Republic* conjures a dialogue between his guru Socrates and his brother Glaucon about the nature of reality. A group of prisoners live in a cave for years with their necks and legs chained so that their gazes are fixed on a wall of the cave. Behind the prisoners a huge fire burns incessantly, and between them and the fire is a raised walkway on which people move carrying different things; the prisoners only see the shadows of the people falling on the wall in front of them. For the prisoners, chained for years, the moving shadows of people are real until their chains are removed and they see the procession of people directly. Plato's parable thus appropriately articulates an age old paradox – whether reality exists by itself or it exists only in the perception of the observer? Everyone claims to know reality and yet we differ on what it is, which is one of the greatest paradoxes of our existence. Is there one reality, but we see it differently or are we unable to see reality in its fullness - our limited faculty capable of grasping only a part of it - and thus creating an illusion of difference? There are several such questions that spring in our mind as soon as we think of reality.

Everything that we perceive through the five senses - the pleasant warmth of the sun, the splash of colours all around, the rustling of leaves, the chirping of birds - appear to be so real that we, in our everyday life, hardly entertain any doubt about their existence. The physical reality around us manifests either in the form of matter or energy. Matter exists as solid, liquid and gas, and there are different forms of energy - light, sound, heat etc. While our ears perceive sound and eyes light, which are different forms of energy, our tongue and nose detect taste and smell respectively, and both these sensations are produced by matter. Only skin has the unique ability to perceive both matter (touch) and energy (heat/cold). Therefore, an understanding of sound, light and matter will provide insights into the nature of reality.

Sound is an Unsound Reality

The ancients knew that sound propagates like a wave. Roman architect and engineer, Marcus Vitruvius, in first century BC, likened sound waves to the motion of ripples on the surface of the water when a stone is thrown into it. Thereafter, virtually nothing happened until the beginning of the seventeenth century when Galileo argued that the pitch of sound was related to its frequency. He reached this conclusion by studying the pattern of sound which was emitted while he was scraping a brass plate with a sharp iron chisel. It is very simple to perform this experiment at home. Take a brass plate and a chisel and scrape the surface of the plate with the chisel. If you move the chisel slowly, no sound will be produced. However, you will hear a clear whistling sound if you increase the speed. You will also notice that the chisel has created a number of marks separated from one another by equal distance along its motion. The width of these marks will be equal to the width of the sharp edge of the chisel and they will be aligned perpendicular to the direction of the motion. If you further increase the speed, the spacing between the marks will reduce and you will hear a sharper whistling sound, a higher tone. The spacing between two marks corresponds to the wavelength of the sound produced. The lesser is the spacing, the lesser the wavelength and the higher the frequency of sound. And the higher the frequency of sound, the higher is the tone.[1]

Around the same time, many scientists attempted to measure the speed of sound, and the first among them were two French polymaths, Pierre Gassendi and Marin Mersenne. Gassendi used a firearm and a flash of light to measure the speed of sound in 1635, which came to be 478 metre per second. The measurement was improved by Mersenne to 450 metre per second but it was still far away from the modern value of 330 metre per second. The value kept improving with better and better measuring techniques. In 1687, Newton, using his newly invented calculus, discovered a formula for calculating the speed of sound in solid, liquid and gas. His formula yielded a value of 979 feet (298 m) per second for the speed of sound in air at sea-level, which was significantly lower than the actual measured value of 1,142 feet (348 m) per second at that time. However, he explained the discrepancy by making allowances for the presence of solid particles and vapour in the air. Newton assumed that the temperature remained constant during compression and rarefaction of the air when sound wave passed through it. This assumption yielded an inaccurate formula, which underestimated the speed of sound. The formula was later suitably modified by Laplace and is now known as Newton-Laplace formula.[2,3]

Scientists from ancient times had some inkling that sound required a medium to travel, but Athanasius Kircher, a German priest and polymath, was the first to conduct an experiment in the year 1650 to test this hypothesis. He kept a bell in a sealed vacuum chamber, which could be activated with the help of a magnet, from outside. When he switched the bell on, he was able to hear the sound coming from inside, which led him to believe that air was not required for the transmission of sound waves. However, people were not convinced. Only ten years later, Robert Boyle, an Anglo-Irish scientist, famous for his law on the relation between pressure and volume of gas, repeated the experiment. He put a ticking watch in a glass jar and sucked the air out with the help of a vacuum pump. The ticking sound grew fainter and fainter when the air was sucked out. Boyle succeeded because Otto von Guericke had invented a vacuum pump in 1654, which was further improved by Robert Hooke. He was able to suck the air from the glass jar more effectively with its help.[4]

How real are the sounds we hear! We know that vibrations produced by any instrument - or our vocal chords - create compressions and rarefactions in the air and the pressure waves travel through air, enter the ear canal, fall upon the eardrums and make them vibrate. The eardrum passes these vibrations through the middle ear bones into the inner ear, called cochlea, which converts the vibrations into electric signals with the help of thousands of tiny hair cells. The electric signals are then transmitted to the brain, which interprets them as sound.

Sound requires a medium to travel; therefore it cannot travel in outer space as there is no atmosphere there. The boundary between earth's atmosphere and outer space is not well-defined because air thins gradually as we go to higher altitude over the surface of the earth. However, Karman line, 100 km above the mean sea level, is generally taken as the beginning of outer space. Beyond that inter-planetary space is largely empty, almost vacuum. When Earth and Venus are closest to each other, the distance between them is 38 million km. Let us imagine a hypothetical sphere with its centre at the centre of the earth and a radius of 38 million km. The volume of this hypothetical sphere is the order of 10^{23} km^3, within which atmosphere exists in a thin spherical shell of thickness 100 km around the surface of the earth with a volume of the order of 10^{11} km^3.* The distance between the Sun and the nearest star Alpha Centauri is 40 trillion km, a million times more than the distance between Earth and Venus, and intergalactic distances are larger by a factor of another million. As the scale becomes larger, the portion where atmosphere exists becomes smaller. Sound, therefore, can be said to exist only in a tiny – almost negligible – part of the vast universe. In vast spaces of the universe, where no atmosphere exists, two persons will not be able to talk to each other. They will have to resort to sign language as if they have suddenly turned deaf and dumb.

Although sound is integral to human experience, it is far from being a universal reality. It exists only in a negligible part of the universe. And human ears are capable of detecting sound waves in a very narrow range of 20-20,000 Hz. (Some dolphins and bats can hear frequencies up to 1,00,000 Hz.)

Light Exists Everywhere, It is Universal

What about colours? Early in our childhood we learn to recognise colours and differentiate between them, but there is no way of knowing whether a colour is perceived similarly by everyone. My 'red' can be different from your 'red'; in

---

*If all the fresh water in rivers and lakes were to correspond to the volume of the hypothetical sphere, then the volume where atmosphere exists would correspond to an average overhead tank of a city water supply system.

fact, I may actually see 'green' when I am shown 'red'. Nobody can enter my mind to find out how I perceive the colour 'red'. As long as I see the three primary colours distinctly I possess normal colour vision; however, inability to distinguish between any two primary colours can be easily detected by using patterns of coloured dots, but even then it would not be possible for anyone to know how I perceive those colours.

Light is reflected from an object, it enters our eyes and after passing through the cornea falls on the retina, which has cells called 'rods' and 'cones'. The cones are stimulated by light of different wavelengths, and they send information to the mind through the optical nerve, which perceives colours. A human eye can see light having wavelengths between 380 and 740 nanometre, but some animals can perceive ultraviolet light with wavelengths less than 380 nm. Therefore, the colours they see though their eyes cannot even be visualised by us as our imagination is limited by the colours we actually see. Thus, light does not possess colours, nor do objects; colour is a creation of the mind. The beautiful colours that surround us, and we think are real do not exist, except in our minds.

Light Consists of Particles, Says Newton, but Huygens Differs

Well, colours may not exist, but light exists, and – unlike sound – it does not require any medium to propagate. It can travel even in vacuum. We see light coming from stars that are billions of light years away, much of its journey taking place through a vast swathe of vacuum. No matter where we are in the universe, stars and galaxies are visible, and in that sense light is very real. Two great scientists of 17th century proposed two radically different theories of light: Christiaan Huygens published *Traité de la lumière* (Treatise on Light) in 1690 arguing that light was a wave whereas Sir Isaac Newton in his 1704 treatise *Opticks* stated that light consisted of very small particles. As a particle was reflected when it fell on any surface, Newton argued, so was light because it consisted of particles. Wave theory explained the reflection of light equally elegantly. It is however in explaining refraction – the phenomenon of bending of light when it propagates from one medium to other – that particle theory and wave theory resorted to different assumptions: While the particle theory asserted that light moved faster in a denser medium, the wave theory claimed exactly the opposite. Newton argued that as light entered a denser medium it experienced an attractive force in a direction perpendicular to the plane separating the two media, which accelerated the light particles in that direction while the component of speed along the separating plane remains unchanged, causing light to bend. Deep inside the denser medium it experienced no net force and therefore it continued to travel in a straight line.

When a stone is thrown in a still pond, ripples move outward in circles of increasing radius. The circles of crests and troughs are called wavefronts. Huygens argued that a beam of light also travelled like ripples in the ponds, but unlike the ripples in the pond, which had circular wavefronts, a parallel beam of light had plane wavefronts. Further, he reasoned that light waves slowed down in a denser medium like water or glass. Therefore, when a parallel beam of light fell at an angle on the surface of glass, it is bent towards a line perpendicular to the surface of glass because one side of the wavefronts hit the glass surface first and thereafter travelled lesser distance in the glass compared to the other end of wavefront that continued to travel in air. Once inside the glass, the wavefronts continued to travel in a straight line.*

---

*The refraction of light is a common everyday phenomenon. Take an empty glass jar and put a coin at the bottom of the jar. Now fill up the jar with water; suddenly it will appear as if the coin is now lying at a lesser depth than earlier.

It was clear that only one of the propositions could be true: Either light travelled faster in a denser medium or it slowed down, but at that time there was no way to measure the speed of light and validate the assertion of either Newton or Huygens. Since light travelled in a straight line, it was natural for Newton to have deduced from his First Law of Motion that it consisted of particles, although collision between two light beams did not lead to their scattering, which would have been the case if light consisted of particles. Further, particle theory was unable to explain the spreading out of light when made to pass through a narrow slit, which was first observed by Francesco Grimaldi in 1665. Wave theory, on the other hand, required a medium for propagation of light and Huygens surmounted this difficulty by assuming that the entire space was permeated with the hypothetical medium called ether, of which there was no experimental confirmation. Both the theories stood on an even keel, but the formidable reputation of Newton tilted the balance in favour of the particle theory and Huygen's theory almost disappeared into obscurity.

Young's Experiment Validates Huygens

The wave theory was resurrected when Thomas Young, an English physicist and polymath, conducted the famous double slit experiment in early 1800s. (Young had actually studied medicine in England and Germany.) A looking glass was placed outside a window to reflect the sunlight towards a small hole in the window shutter. The horizontal light beam coming into the room after passing through the pinhole was split into two by a slip of card about one thirtieth of an inch in breadth. Young observed the shadow of the slip card on several screens kept on a table opposite the pinhole and found that while the centre of the shadow was always white, it was accompanied by similar parallel fringes of smaller sizes, and the number of fringes depended upon the distance at which the shadow was observed.[5] If particle theory of light was indeed valid, only two bright spots should have been observed in the shadow irrespective of the position of the screen. Young's explanation was prescient:

> From the experiments and calculations which have been premised, we may be allowed to infer, that homogeneous light, at certain equal distances in the direction of its motion, is possessed of opposite qualities, capable of neutralising or destroying each other, and of extinguishing the light, where they happen to be united; that these qualities succeed each other alternately in successive concentric superficies, at distances which are constant for the same light, passing through the same medium.... But, since we know that sound diverges in concentric superficies, and that musical sounds consist of opposite qualities, capable of neutralising each other, and succeeding at certain equal intervals, which are different according to the difference of the note, we are fully authorised to conclude, that there must be some strong resemblance between the nature of sound and that of light.[6]

Let me illustrate this with an example: Imagine you are standing at a point P in a pond, which is at a distance of 10 metres from another point Q. Now imagine another point R in the pond, in close vicinity of Q, such that the distance PR is 10.5 metres. Two stones are now simultaneously thrown in the pond which land at the point Q and R respectively. Assume that the waves move at speed of one metre per second and the distance between two successive crests or troughs is also one metre. Therefore, the wave crests emanating from the point Q will hit you every second, beginning from 10th second and troughs from point R will reach P every second, starting from 11th second, neutralising the crests coming from Q. In short, you will appear to stand in still water. However, at some other points, where path difference between QP and RP is zero or in multiples of wavelength (one metre), the waves from the two points will reinforce each other. If you travel on the circumference of an imaginary circle with its centre at Q, in some segments of the circumference you will encounter no waves, while in others they would be reinforced. This is exactly what Young observed: Alternate white and dark fringes.

The double slit experiment should have settled the century old debate on the nature of light, but the proponents of corpuscular theory remained sceptical. They were unwilling to abandon the long cherished belief in Newton's theory until as late as 1850, when finally Leon Foucault, a French Physicist, struck at its very heart by experimentally demonstrating that light travelled slower in water than air. Further confirmation came 15 years later when James Clerk Maxwell formulated a set of equations that unified electricity, magnetism and light. "It seems we have strong reason to conclude," he wrote, "that light itself (including radiant heat, and other radiations, if any) is an electromagnetic disturbance in the form of waves propagated through the electromagnetic field according to electromagnetic laws."[7] Huygen's wave theory received widespread recognition after a lapse of 160 years from when it was first proposed though a critical element of the jigsaw puzzle was still missing. For the proponents of wave theory - from Huygens to Maxwell - ether was the hypothetical medium that carried light waves. Since light travelled even through vacuum, it was supposed to fill everything, even vacuum. Maxwell wrote:

> We have therefore some reason to believe, from the phenomena of light and heat, that there is an ethereal medium filling space and permeating bodies, capable of being set in motion and of transmitting that motion from one part to another, and of communicating that motion to gross matter so as to heat it and affect it in various ways.[8]

His equations yielded a constant c, the speed at which electromagnetic waves travelled and its value was very nearly the speed of light – and therefore he concluded that light was nothing but a type of electromagnetic wave. The constancy of c fitted well with the idea of ether. After all if light always travelled with speed c, it must be with respect to something, and that something was ether, which was all pervading. However, any evidence of the existence of ether was hard to come by.

Search for Ether, Medium for the Transmission of Light

From 1881, Albert Michelson, the first American to receive the Nobel Prize in sciences, started conducting a series of experiments, initially alone, but later with another American, Edward Morley, to confirm the existence of ether. The underlying idea behind the experiment was pretty simple. We know that if two cars are moving with the same speed in the same direction, the relative speed between them is zero, that is, the person sitting in one car finds that the other car is stationary with respect to him. Conversely, if the cars are travelling with the same speed in opposite directions, the relative speed between the two cars is doubled. The earth revolves around the sun with a speed of approximately 30 km per second, and therefore if a light ray is emitted in the direction of earth's movement, the ray will move with respect to the earth at a speed slightly less than the speed of light relative to the ether. Similarly, if the light ray travels in the direction opposite to the movement of earth, its speed will be slightly more than the speed of light relative to the ether. Michelson, however, erroneously thought that a ray travelling in a direction perpendicular to the motion of the earth would not be affected – a mistake that was pointed out independently by Alfred Potier and HA Lorentz, and which was subsequently corrected by Michelson. He explained the concept to his children with amazing simplicity:

> Two beams of light race against each other, like two swimmers, one struggling upstream and back, while the

other, covering the same distance, just crosses the river and returns. The second swimmer will always win, if there is any current in the river.[9]

This can be explained with an example: Suppose there is a motorboat in a river that is 50 metres wide. If there is no current in the river and the boat moves with a speed of 5 metres/second, it will take 20 seconds for the boat to cross the river and come back, and in the same time the boat can also travel a distance of 50 metres upstream and return. However, if a current is flowing with a speed of 3 m/s, it will take 25 s to cover the same distance upstream and only 6.25 s to return, that is, a total time of 31.25 s. The river is flowing from the north to the south and you are at a place X on the western bank. In order to reach a point Y on the eastern bank, which is right across X, you will have to steer the boat in north-eastern direction. The time taken to cross the river from X to Y and vice versa can be calculated with the help of little trigonometry, which comes to 12.5 s each. Therefore, the time taken to cross the river and come back, that is, 25 s, is less than 31.25 s taken to go upstream and return.

The most accurate measurement of light at that time had an error margin of 50 km per second[10], and therefore it was not possible to directly detect small variations in the speed of light due to movement of the earth. Michelson designed an apparatus that split a single beam of light into two with the help of a half-silvered mirror, and then one beam of light travelled in the direction of the motion of the earth, while the other travelled perpendicular to it. The two beams were reflected back and made to combine with each other in order to produce interference pattern, much like Young's double slit experiment. He expected the interferences fringes to shift because of the earth's motion when he rotated the apparatus by 90 degree, but the fringe shift was almost negligible. The experiment failed to detect any motion of the earth relative to the ether, which could only be possible if the earth dragged the ether as it moved around the sun.

But 'ether drag hypothesis' was incompatible with the stellar aberration observed by James Bradley. A telescope should be slightly tilted and not be directly pointed towards a star in order to observe it, much in the same manner as one has to keep one's umbrella tilted while running in the rain. The apparent shift in the position of a star would not be possible if the earth dragged the ether along with it. The hypothetical ether did not lose much currency despite these contradictions and the fact that a nearly impossible set of qualities were demanded from it – it had to be highly rigid in order to support light wave travelling with super-fast speed, and yet it had to allow the movement of planets through it.[11]

HA Lorentz and George FitzGerald sought to explain the negative result of Michelson-Morley experiment, without abandoning the concept of stationary ether, by arguing that the length of an object contracted in the direction of the motion. They claimed that the ether was stationary but fringe pattern did not shift as expected in Michelson-Morley experiment because the distance between two mirrors in the direction of the earth's motion contracted, and consequently there was no time delay between the two beams – one travelling in the direction of earth's motion and the other perpendicular to it – when they recombined to produce interference fringes. Scientists were as reluctant to discard the ether as they were to abandon the corpuscular theory of light, but Lorentz-FitzGerald contraction and subsequent works of Henri Poincare paved the way for special theory of relativity, which was proposed by Albert Einstein in 1905 doing away with the idea of ether altogether.

Dual Nature of Light

In 1899, JJ Thomson discovered that a negatively charged particle is ejected when ultraviolet light – light of frequency higher than visible light – shines on certain metals. The phenomenon of emission of electrons from a metal when irradiated with light was called *photoelectric effect*. Three years later, in 1902, Philipp Lenard, a German physicist, while studying the photoelectric effect, stumbled upon startling results: The electrons were not ejected unless the metal was illuminated with light above a threshold frequency. Although a bright light source ejected more electrons from the metal than a dim light source of same frequency, the maximum speed with which the electrons left the metal plate did not depend on the intensity of light. A dimmer source of higher frequency produced electrons with higher speed than a brighter source of lower frequency. Lenard, however, could not provide any convincing explanation for the results.

But Einstein was quick to realise that it was not possible to explain the behaviour of the electrons in Lenard's experiment without abandoning the established view of light being a wave. In one of the four papers titled "Concerning an Heuristic Point of View toward the Emission and Transformation of Light" submitted in the year 1905, Einstein proposed that light consisted of quanta of energy, later named as photons:

> The usual conception, that the energy of light is continuously distributed over the space through which it propagates, encounters very serious difficulties when one attempts to explain the photoelectric phenomena, as has been pointed out in Herr Lenard's pioneering paper ... however, one can conceive of the ejection of electrons by light in the following way. Energy quanta penetrate into the surface layer of the body, and their energy is transformed, at least in part, into kinetic energy of electrons. The simplest way to imagine this is that a light quantum delivers its entire energy to a single electron: we shall assume that this is what happens. The possibility should not be excluded, however, that electrons might receive their energy only in part from the light quantum.[12]

The energy quantum of light depends on the frequency of light - higher the frequency, higher the energy. It is indeed paradoxical that the energy possessed by a light particle (photon) depends on the frequency or wavelength of light, which is a property of waves. Therefore, a photon of higher frequency will dislodge an electron with higher speed, as was observed by Lenard. Increasing the intensity of light means that the source is emitting more photons per second, but if an individual photon does not have sufficient energy to dislodge an electron, bombarding the metal piece with more such photons does not help. Einstein's proposition explained why light above certain threshold frequency dislodged electrons from the metal surface. It was inconceivable that light could behave sometimes like a particle and sometimes like a wave, but the scientific investigation conducted over more than 200 years - from Huygens's *Traité de la lumière* published in 1690 to Einstein's photoelectric paper in 1905 - culminated in paradoxical wave-particle duality of light, although it was not fully accepted until 1923 when Arthur Compton demonstrated that the collision between a photon and an electron was exactly like the collision between two billiard balls. Einstein got the Nobel Prize for the photoelectric effect in 1922, a year before his theory was confirmed by Compton's scattering experiment.

When a billiard ball hits another ball, which is stationary, the stationary ball gains some momentum while the striking ball loses some. From the laws of conservation of momentum and energy, the speeds of the balls after collision can be calculated. In a collision between a photon and an electron, the photon loses some energy and hence the wavelengths of the scattered photons are larger than striking photons. Compton derived the formula for the change in wavelength of the photons by the laws of conservation of momentum and energy, which matched the experimental observations.

Matter Behaves Like a Wave

Besides sound and light, we perceive another form of energy, that is, heat, through our skin. But heat, like light, is a type of electromagnetic radiation. While visible light (visible to human eyes) occupies a narrow range of spectrum with wavelengths from 380 to 740 nanometre, the spectrum of heat radiation is much broader – 100 nanometre to 10,000 nanometre. Barring this, there is no difference between heat and light; both are electromagnetic waves.

We now turn to matter, the second pillar of physical reality. Everything around us exists in the form of matter, including our body. Therefore, people from ancient times have been curious about the nature and composition of matter. They thought that the smallest indivisible unit of matter could be obtained by repeatedly dividing it, which they called atom. The next chapter will go into the details of the structure of the atom. For now, we skip that and proceed to a discovery about the nature of matter, which had far-reaching consequences.

In 1924, two years after Einstein got the Nobel Prize, a French physicist, Louis de Broglie, in his PhD thesis, submitted that all matter exhibited wave characteristics, and the wavelength of matter waves was inversely proportional to its mass and speed. But matter wave is unlike any other type of wave we have so far known. A wave is a variation of some measurable attribute that travels in space and time: pressure in case of sound wave and electric and magnetic field in light. And therefore a question naturally arises: What is the parameter whose variation constitutes matter wave? Unfortunately, de Broglie did not provide any answer to this question, and it was not until Erwin Schrodinger, a brilliant Austrian Physicist, formally presented a set of equations in 1926 describing matter wave mathematically that any physical meaning could be attributed to it. He submitted four papers that laid the foundation of quantum physics to the same journal *Annalen der physik* in which Einstein had published his papers - and therefore it would not be an exaggeration to claim that 1926 was an extraordinary year for Schrodinger as the year 1905 was for Einstein.

The wave function associated with a particle represents, Schrodinger argued, the variation of density of the particle over the wave packet.[13] In other words, the particle does not exist at a single point but is smeared all over the wave function. Schrodinger's interpretation of his own equation therefore almost sounded the death knell for the particle. The proposition was deeply troubling as by that time "it was already possible to count particles [smallest one like electrons] by means of scintillations or with a Geiger counter, and to photograph their tracks with the aid of a Wilson cloud chamber."[14] That the particle existed as a continuous density distribution instead of a point mass was not borne out by these observations. Fortunately, in the very same year, Max Born came up with another interpretation of Schrodinger's equation, which is now widely accepted as the correct description of wave function. He suggested that the wave function associated with a particle represented the probability of finding the particle at any point in space and time.[15] Therefore, the matter wave was not an undulation of some real physical quantity like other types of waves, rather it was a probability wave.

Mathematical representation of matter wave and its physical interpretation were significant milestones in enunciating the wave nature of particle, and that they were achieved within two years of de Broglie's hypothesis indicates how quickly the fundamentals of quantum mechanics were being laid out. However, clinching evidence in the support of wave-particle duality of matter could only come from experimental observations, which happened sooner than later in the year 1927. Two American physicists, CL Davisson and LH Germer, had been studying the impact of electrons on nickel surface since 1919. They expected the electrons to get scattered uniformly in all directions after impinging on the nickel surface because even a smooth looking surface would be too rough for particles as small as electrons. Imagine throwing a stream of balls on a bumpy surface; the balls will be reflected in all directions. The observations of the experiment were in agreement with the assumption, but during the course of one such experiment air accidentally entered into the vacuum chamber in which the electrons from a heated filament were accelerated and allowed to strike the target oxidising the metal surface. To deoxidise nickel, it was heated in a high temperature oven and the experiment was resumed. To their utter surprise, the electrons were not found to be uniformly scattered, but showed distinct peak at a particular angle that varied with the speed of the colliding electrons.[16]

Please recall Young's double slit experiment in which a beam of light was split into two and they were made to interfere with each other producing bright and dark fringes. The waves can reinforce or cancel one another when they meet. Davisson and Germer argued that the heating of nickel at high temperature made it coalesce into a single crystal – a material in which atoms are arranged in a regular pattern. When the electrons collided with the target at high speed, some were reflected from the upper layer of atoms and some penetrated the nickel surface only to be reflected by the second layer of atoms. The reflected electrons then travelled to the electron detector where they reinforced or cancelled each other, just like waves do, producing distinct maxima and minima. Davisson and Germer calculated the wavelength of the electron wave by de Broglie formula, that is, $\lambda = h/mv$, where λ is wavelength, h is Planck's constant, m is mass and v speed of the particle. The speed with which electrons collided with the target was 4,390 km per second, from which a value of 0.166 nanometre for the wavelength was derived. The electron detector recorded highest intensity of electrons at an angle of 50° from the incident beam and the distance between atomic planes was known to be 0.091 nanometre. By using Bragg equation for maxima in diffraction pattern, the wavelength was calculated to be 0.165 nanometre; the observed wavelength, therefore, agreed with the de Broglie wavelength confirming the hypothesis.[17] Davisson succinctly observed:

> The electron as a particle is too well established to be discredited by a few experiments with a nickel crystal. The most we are apt to allow is that there are circumstances in which it is more convenient to regard electrons as waves than as particles. We will allow perhaps that electrons have a dual nature - when they produce tracks in a CTR Wilson cloud experiment they are particles, but when they are scattered by a crystal they are waves.[18]

Compton experiment demonstrated particle like nature of waves and Davisson experiment confirmed the wave like nature of particles, providing irrefutable evidence of wave particle duality. Since then experiments have been conducted with larger particles like protons, neutrons, and even atoms and molecules and they all have exhibited wave like characteristics. Larger everyday objects like a cricket ball has too small a wavelength to be detected by any experiment. Despite these breakthroughs, quantum mechanics remained a highly contentious subject throughout the decade of 1920s, and the scientists sparred with one another, often acrimoniously, over the various interpretations of quantum mechanics. While Niels Bohr, Werner Heisenberg, Max Born and others supported the probabilistic interpretation of quantum mechanics, Albert Einstein, Erwin Schrodinger and others expressed serious misgivings. The Fifth Solvay International Conference held in October 1927, where many eminent physicists assembled to discuss the newly formulated quantum theory, witnessed some of the intellectually most challenging debates on the subject, at the end of which Bohr's interpretation - later known as Copenhagen interpretation of quantum mechanics - was largely accepted.

The proponents of Copenhagen interpretation argued that the probability wave associated with a particle collapsed as soon as the particle was observed and therefore it was detected at a particular point in space and time. To Einstein and others, the idea that reality manifested only through the agency of a conscious observer appeared quite disturbing. They were intuitively convinced that the world was a more definitive place to live than was revealed by quantum mechanics. In a letter to Max Born on 4th December 1926, Einstein had reflected this concern: "Quantum mechanics is certainly imposing. But an inner voice tells me that it is not yet the real thing. The theory says a lot, but does not really bring us any closer to the secret of the 'old one'. I, at any rate, am convinced that He [God] is not playing at dice."[19] Einstein never fully reconciled to the Copenhagen interpretation, often proposing several thought experiments to discredit it.

Although the Solvay conference greatly enhanced the understanding of quantum mechanics, it also raised several questions. If, how and when wave function collapses remains a fiercely contested issue even now and the scientists are no closer to resolving it. Imagine electrons passing through a very tiny hole and falling on a plate that emits a flash of light whenever an electron strikes it. Does the wave function collapse when the electron strikes the plate? Or does it collapse when the flash of light reaches the eyes, or in the optical nerve or in the visual cortex? Or is it that it collapses when it encounters human consciousness? Who is observing and what is being observed? How do we separate the observer from the observed?

The plate consists of atoms, and they are made of protons, neutrons and electrons - all quantum particles, but so are our eyes, the optical nerve, and the visual cortex. They all follow the same rules of quantum mechanics. The electron travels like a wave, but arrives at the plate like a particle. The photons travelling from the plate to our eyes also exhibit the same wave-particle duality. The photoreceptors – rods and cones – in the retina transmit the image to the brain through optical nerves by electrical signals. In this complex process of observing how do we arbitrarily decide the boundary between the observer and the observed?

Alternative Interpretations of Quantum Mechanics

In 1956, Huge Everett, an American physicist proposed in his doctoral thesis "The Theory of the Universal Wave Function" what is now known as 'many-worlds interpretation' of quantum mechanics. As per Copenhagen interpretation, a particle exists in a superposition of several states of being at the same time until it is measured – the act of measuring leading to the collapse of the wave function. An electron can be at two places at the same time but it is found to be at only one location when its position is actually measured. Everett discarded the observer induced collapse of the wave function proposed by the Copenhagen interpretation and argued that one particular outcome was not preferred over another. While the electron was found to be in one of the states when measured, it also manifested simultaneously in all other possible states in other universes. At every event the universe splits into as many universes as there are possible outcomes. While a person detects the electron in one state in this universe, a copy of him detects it in another state in another universe. In his model, the observer is not distinct from what is being observed; rather observer is also split into many in order to observe all possible outcomes in different universes. Although the many-worlds interpretation did not find much favour among the scientists, it remains a powerful thought even today.

There are other theories, notably Bohm's hidden variable theory, which accepted the validity of the quantum mechanics but argued that it was an incomplete description of reality. Bohm's theory, an extension of the abandoned idea of de Broglie, attempted to restore determinism at quantum scale by arguing that "there would indeed be some definite reality, but the parameters which precisely define a system would not be directly accessible to us...."[20] Since the alternate theories did not get widespread recognition and the Copenhagen interpretation continues to remain the mainstay of quantum mechanics, we return to the central question of collapse of the wave function.

Hungarian physicist, Eugene Wigner claimed that since all measuring apparatuses themselves existed in superposed quantum states because they were nothing but conglomeration of quantum particles, the collapse of the wave function "takes place whenever the result of an observation enters the consciousness of the observer - or, to be even more painfully precise, my own consciousness, since I am the only observer, all other people being only subjects of my observations."[21] The wave function collapses only when it encounters a non-physical reality called consciousness. But whose consciousness is enough for causing the collapse? Can an ant or a cat cause the collapse or only human beings have this privilege? Why and how does this collapse happen? Sadly there are no answers to these questions as we do not know what consciousness is.

The objects that we see and feel around us give a concrete shape to our sense of reality, which is threatened, if not altogether destroyed, by quantum mechanics. It is natural to expect that the constituents of objects around us are real no matter how much we divide them, but the idea of reality becomes very fuzzy at the microscopic level. Matter exists only as probability waves until it is observed. If Wigner is to be believed, the probability waves assume material form only when they enter our consciousness - and there is no way to either confirm or refute it. But regardless of where exactly the wave function collapses, the idea of reality completely independent of a conscious observer is untenable. After all, a chair and a table can exist side by side without the chair being aware of the existence of the table or vice versa.

Wigner argued that there were two kinds of reality: the content of consciousness and the physical world. The physical world was constructed in the mind of the observer only through the content of consciousness and therefore the nature of universal realities could not be fully understood without knowing the content of consciousness:

> The fact that the first kind of reality (ie consciousness) is absolute and ... that we discuss the realities of the second kind (perceived objects) much more, may lead to the impression that the first kind of reality is something very simple. We all know that this is not the case. On the contrary, the content of the consciousness is something very complicated and it is my impression that not even the psychologists can give a truly adequate picture of it ... the inadequacy of our appreciation of its properties may be one of the most potent barriers against establishing the nature of universal realities at the present time.[22]

Humans cannot see ultraviolet light but some animals can. The physical world surely exists but the form in which it is perceived is determined by the content of consciousness. It is entirely plausible that a different 'content of consciousness' could see the same physical world differently. What then can be said about the universal reality – the reality that cannot be fully described, let alone be comprehended, despite centuries of rigorous scientific inquiry?

Various Schools of Hindu Philosophy

The true nature of reality has been no less contentious a subject – and equally stimulating – in Hindu philosophy. It is, therefore, not surprising that various schools of Hindu philosophy produced a very wide range of thoughts in order to make sense of the world that they lived in. Carvaka, the founder of materialist school of philosophy known as *lokayata,* accorded absolute primacy to the reality perceived by the five senses. His precise origin is shrouded in controversy – the matter being made worse by near total discontinuity of the tradition after twelfth century AD leaving only fragments of the knowledge.[23] He considered any reality other than what could be perceived by the senses as non-existent. He believed that everything was made up of only four elements: Earth, water, fire and air and various combinations of these elements produced different objects and they could be reduced ultimately to these four basic elements.

He made no differentiation between gross body and subtle consciousness and claimed that consciousness emanated from the body itself. He argued that nobody had ever proved the existence of consciousness independent from the body – when a person died, his consciousness ceased to exist – therefore distinguishing it as a separate entity was without any evidence. But he could not provide any explanation as to why some objects possessed consciousness while the others did not; after all the material world can only be perceived by consciousness which according to Carvaka is a property derived from matter.

Is reality what we perceive from our senses or is that mere manifestation of reality and not reality itself? A bowl of liquid is kept in front of us; we touch it, see it, taste it and conclude that it is water. We identify water by its properties. Ice differs in its properties with water and is perceived differently by our senses although they consist of same molecules. The manner in which the molecules combine determines the properties of resultant matter. It is, therefore, natural to ask what is real: Water or its molecules. The molecules in turn are made up of atoms, atoms of protons, neutrons and electrons and so on. We can keep dividing the matter to understand the fundamental reality of nature, but we unravel one layer of the reality only to be confounded by another layer of it, forcing us to ultimately abandon the purely materialistic approach to reality.

Samkhya school of philosophy realized this limitation of Carvaka's materialism, which considered consciousness as a derivative of matter. Matter can be divided almost endlessly; it can be touched, smelt and seen but consciousness can neither be divided nor be touched, nor smelt and nor seen. *Samkhya* school therefore contended that matter (*prakriti*) and consciousness (*purusha*) were different entities and a fuller understanding of reality was not possible without exploring consciousness. Swami Krishnananda explains beautifully:

> The world is not as it appears to the eyes; it is a whitewash that we see, as the inside bricks and the cement are not visible to the outer perception. *Samkhya* goes deep into the categorisation of the principles of the universe, and starts its argument from the very consciousness that tries to make any investigation at all: Who is it that is trying to make an investigation into the nature of the world? Who is it that wants to know anything at all? It is me. Now, what kind of me is it?[24]

The material world can be said to exist only for a conscious observer capable of perceiving it in some form; although there could be a vast difference between what actually exists and how its existence is perceived, there is no way of knowing what exactly is the material world that surrounds us. We do not really see any object with our eyes; rather what we see is the reflection of light from the objects. Naturally, we are not able to see anything in pitch darkness. We do not know whether the image of an object that is formed on the retina of our eyes precisely denotes the object under observation or whether the image that is formed on the retina is faithfully transmitted to the brain. The eyes, the retina, the brain all are material entities and we can keep on moving further to know where actually the object is perceived until we encounter consciousness. Therefore, it would not be an exaggeration to say that in some sense it is the consciousness that brings the world into existence.

Vedanta and the Four States of Consciousness

Vedanta school believes that the *Brahman* - indivisible, infinite and universal consciousness - is the ultimate reality, but it manifests in different forms. In the waking state, the consciousness manifests as *vishva* - everyday reality that confronts us. Our senses enjoy the gross external world in this state. In the dreaming state, the consciousness manifests as *taijasa* and it enjoys the subtle dream objects. In deep sleep, our consciousness is not only cut off from the external world but it is also bereft of all dreams - this state is called *prajna*. *Vishva* is the gross reality, *taijasa* the subtle reality and *prajna* is the bliss.

Common sense considers dream world to be unreal - an illusion that comes to an end as soon as our consciousness awakes. "We regard, usually, dreams to be consequences of waking perception, and it is held that the objects seen in dream[s] are psychological rather than physical. We come in contact with real objects in the waking state, but we contact only imagined things in the dream state. While there is actual satisfaction, actual pleasure and actual pain in the waking world, there is an imagined pleasure, imagined satisfaction and imagined pain in the dream world. While the objects of the waking world are not our creation, the objects of the dream world are our own mental creation."[25] The entire notion of space and time is distorted in the dreaming state and the events defy the laws of physics, something that is impossible in the real world. The physical world is publically shared, but the dream world is an individual experience. The transience of the dream world is further reinforced by the fact that a person can be deliberately woken up from the dream world to the predictable real world, but not the other way round.

Vedanta challenges this commonly held notion by arguing that the dream world appears to be as real while in the dream as the real world appears in the waking state. Assume a stationary railroad car on the two ends of which two bullets are fired simultaneously as seen by an observer standing in the car. A second railroad car is moving on the same rail away from the first car at a constant velocity and another observer standing on the moving car sees the bullets fired from the first car, but surprisingly he notices that the two bullets were not fired simultaneously. The two observers do not agree on the simultaneity of the events because they are in different frames of reference.

Vedanta argues that the waking state and the dream state are two different frames of reference and therefore the observers see the reality differently in different states. No observer can be standing simultaneously in both the stationary car and the moving car and therefore they will never agree on the duration between the firing of two bullets. Similarly, nobody can be both sleeping and awake at the same time, and therefore to call one reality real and consider the other reality as illusion would be erroneous.

Sigmund Freud, the father of psychoanalysis, admitted that "dreams, as everyone knows, may be confused, unintelligible, or positively nonsensical; what they say may contradict all that we know of reality; and we behave in them like insane people, since, so long as we are dreaming, we attribute objective reality to the contents of the dream."[26]

The argument that the contents of the dream are not real – at least in the reference frame of waking state – is *prima facie* persuasive, but it is equally true that the fear, the anxiety, the excitement experienced by the dreamer is real: Haven't we woken up from a nightmare sweating profusely.

Moreover, several studies have confirmed that some dreams foretell future events. If dreams are completely unreal, how do they foretell events happening in the real world? Do dreams appear illusory because we are mostly in the waking state? Would our perception of dreams change if we were mostly dreaming? Suppose we were dreaming 23 hours in a day and were awake only for an hour, would that make a difference in the way we perceive dreams? Sadly, these tantalizing questions remain in the realm of philosophical speculation.

The consciousness manifests as *taijasa* - subtle reality - in the dreaming state, and *Vedanta* not only considers the dream reality to be as real as the waking reality but also a higher form of reality than *Vishva*. The third state of consciousness - *prajna* or bliss - is experienced during the deep sleep (*sushupti*), "where - *nakancana kaamam kaamayate* - one desires nothing, because the mind has withdrawn itself from both the physical and subtle objects. *Na kancana svapnam pashyati:* It does not dream also, because even psychic activity has ceased. *Tatsushuptam:* This is complete absorption of the mind into itself. But this absorption is of an unconscious nature."[27] In deep sleep, there is no anxiety, no fear, no pain; the mind is at complete rest.

It is the content of consciousness that determines the form in which it manifests in the different states, being most proliferous in the waking state and most undifferentiated in the deep sleep. *Prajna* is a higher state of reality than *taijasa* because the consciousness is in its purer form. The three states of consciousness described thus far are commonly experienced by us, but there is a fourth state called *turiya* - which literally means fourth. In *turiya*, the consciousness is neither directed towards the external world nor towards the internal dream world. An object has some mass, it occupies some volume and it is defined by some features, but *turiya* displays no such properties. It cannot be seen; it cannot be grasped; and it cannot be defined, let alone be measured. It is pure consciousness sans any accompaniment. The world, which is an illusory manifestation of consciousness, ceases to be in *turiya*. The ego disappears and all duality ceases to exist. The boundary between 'I' and rest of the universe fades. This is the state the *yogis* strive to attain through *sadhana*.

Many psychoanalytical researchers have shown that children begin to differentiate between the dream and the waking reality sometimes during the third or fourth year.[28] It is also well known that we are not born with an ego and our sense of having a self, distinct from the rest of the world, evolves during infancy and early childhood.[29] Therefore, it is entirely plausible that children's ability to distinguish between dream and reality is in some way related to the development of ego.

> Do you know who you were before you were born? No, because nothing is remembered except the ego, and the ego takes three to five years to develop. Therefore, the psychologists say that we cannot remember our lives before the age of three to five years. Why is this so? After all, we were present from birth to the age of three. It is because it takes three years for the ego to develop.... Children never hesitate to steal or tell lies. This does not mean [that] they are thieves or liars. The actual fact is, the ego is still absent so the child cannot differentiate between 'mine' and 'thine'. What we look upon as theft is pure socialism to a child.... We often see a child waking up from sleep crying because of a doll that was broken in his dreams. The ego is essential to differentiate between the dreams of the night and the reality of the day.[30]

The different states of consciousness can be likened to the different states of matter. Most objects around us are solid. We differentiate between them on the basis of their shape, size, colour etc. Liquids are not as numerous as solids in our everyday life; and gases even less so. Oxygen, nitrogen and carbon dioxide are present in the atmosphere, but our senses cannot distinguish one from the other. Only gases with distinct odours can be recognised by human senses. Yet we know that solid, liquid and gas are different states of the same matter. If solid is heated, it turns into liquid, and then into gas. At very high temperature gas becomes plasma, a hot soup of electrons and ions, which is called the fourth state of matter. It is interesting that although more than 99% of matter in the universe today exists in the form of plasma, we are least aware of it in our day to day life. The universe in the early stage was a uniform hot soup of atomic nuclei and electrons and as it expanded and cooled gradually, numerous galaxies, stars and planets were formed paving the way for appearance of varieties of liquids and solids that we see today.

Of the five senses through which we perceive the world, sound, sight and touch play the most significant role in shaping our understanding of reality. The fact that we can talk to, see and bump into each other provides the most authoritative definition of everyday ubiquitous reality. It was therefore entirely apposite to begin our investigation of reality by trying to understand the nature of light, but two hundred years of research by the physicists ended up in confusion as to whether light is a particle or wave, forcing them to finally recognise the dual nature of light. But more startlingly, it was found that the sturdiest pillar on which our perception of everyday reality rests, that is matter, exists as probability wave. Although there is no consensus as to where and how a probability wave collapses, the role of a conscious observer in the collapse of wave function is hard to refute. The search of reality ultimately gets mired in the quicksand of consciousness, a non-material entity.

Quite the reverse, philosophy begins its arguments from consciousness. Who is capable of asking a question such as what is reality? Therefore, reality has no meaning outside the consciousness of the observer. "An ant's perception may not be the same as an elephant's perception, and so on. The judgment of values varies in accordance with the capacity to perceive in the case of different species of creation. The human being is one species, and he cannot take upon himself the privilege of knowing everything as if he is omniscient. He has only human eyes, and therefore, he sees only human values, and can see nothing else in this world."[31] Consciousness is the ultimate reality. All that was non-existent in the beginning and which will not exist in the end cannot be said to exist in between. The dream world disappears as soon as consciousness returns to the waking state. Similarly, the cosmos dissolves when consciousness attains the state of *turiya*.

Science begins its search from matter, philosophy from consciousness. Science neatly explains reality until it encounters consciousness and philosophy's contention that matter is an illusory creation of consciousness cannot be tested by scientific methods. Both struggle to provide a complete picture of reality. It is possible that a conscious being like us although capable of asking questions about consciousness cannot fully understand it. The world may be an illusion. Consciousness may not exist independent of matter.

Our understanding of the fundamental nature of reality has been enriched over the centuries by the work of outstanding people and the boundary of human knowledge may expand even further, but science has been unable to develop a theory of consciousness, and it is doubtful that it will be ever able to probe the essence of consciousness. Science may reach closer, and yet reality can continue to defy it in many unexpected ways. Perhaps it was this realisation – not borne out of failure but sheer futility – that turned Wigner to seek solace in philosophy in his late years. "The full meaning of life, the collective meaning of all human desires, is fundamentally a mystery beyond our grasp. As a young man, I chafed at this state of affairs. But by now I have made peace with it. I even feel a certain honour to be associated with such a mystery."[32]

Notes and References

1. *Dialogue Concerning Two New Sciences by Galileo Galilei*, translated by Henry Crew and Alfonso de Salvio, pp 101-2, Cosimo Classics, New York, 2010.
2. *Springer Handbook of Acoustics*, edited by Thomas D Rossing, second edition, pp 12-3, Springer-Verlag, Berlin, 2015.
3. *Mathematical Principles of Natural Philosophy* by Sir Isaac Newton, p 369, translated by Andrew Motte, First American edition, Daniel Adee, New York, 1848.
4. "Acoustics and Optics" by Paolo Mancosu in *The Cambridge History of Science*, Volume 3, *Early Modern Science*, edited by Roy Porter, Katharine Park and Lorraine Daston, pp 609-10, Cambridge University Press, 2006.
5. The Bakerian Lecture: "Experiments and Calculations Relative to Physical Optics", Thomas Young, *Philosophical Transactions* of the Royal Society of London, Vol 94, 1804, pp 1-16.
6. *Ibid*, pp 11-2.
7. "A Dynamical Theory of the Electromagnetic Field", James Clerk Maxwell, *Philosophical Transactions* of the Royal Society of London, Vol 155, 1865, p 466.
8. *Ibid*, p 460.
9. *The Master of Light: A Biography of Albert A Michelson* by Dorothy Livingston, p 77, The University of Chicago Press, Chicago, 1979.
10. *Ibid*, p 59.
11. *A History of the Theories of Aether and Electricity* by ET Whittaker, p 128, Dover Publications, Inc, New York, 1951.
12. "Einstein's Proposal of the Photon Concept – a translation of the Annalen der Physik Paper of 1905", AB Arons and MB Peppard, *American Journal of Physics*, Vol 33, No 5, May 1965, pp 367-74.
13. "The Statistical Interpretation of Quantum Mechanics", Max Born, in *Nobel Lectures in Physics (1942-1962)*, p 261, World Scientific, Singapore, 1998.

14. *Ibid*, p 261.
15. *Ibid*, p 262.
16. *Concepts of Modern Physics* by Arthur Beiser, p 104, Tata McGraw Hill Education, Sixth edition, New Delhi, 2008.
17. *Ibid*, p 105.
18. "The Diffraction of Electrons by a Crystal of Nickel", CJ Davisson, *Bell System Technical Journal*, Vol 7, No 1, 1928, p 105.
19. *The Born-Einstein Letters: Correspondence between Albert Einstein and Max and Hedwig Born from 1916 to 1955*, translated by Irene Born, p 91, The McMillan Press Ltd, London, 1971.
20. *The Emperor's New Mind: Concerning Computers, Minds and the Laws of Physics* by Roger Penrose, p 362, Vintage, London, 1990.
21. *The Collected Works of Eugene P Wigner*, edited by Jagdish Mehra, Part B, Volume 6, p 265, Springer-Verlag, Berlin, 1995.
22. *Ibid*, p 263.
23. *Studies on the Carvaka Lokayata*, Ramkrishna Bhattacharya, p 65, Anthem Press, London, 2011.
24. *Commentary on the Bhagavadgita* by Swami Krishnananda, p 40, The Divine Life Society, Rishikesh, India. https://www.swami-krishnananda.org/bgita/Commentary_Bhagavadgita.pdf (accessed on 26th October 2017)
25. *The Mandukya Upanishad*, Swami Krishnananda, p 68, The Divine Life Society, Rishikesh, India. https://www.swami-krishnananda.org/mand/Mandukya_Upanishad.pdf (accessed on 26th October 2017)
26. As quoted in *Dreams, Illusion and other Realities by Wendy Doniger O'Flaherty*, p 42, The University of Chicago Press, Chicago, 1986.
27. *The Mandukya Upanishad*, Swami Krishnananda, p 86, The Divine Life Society, Rishikesh, India. https://www.swami-krishnananda.org/mand/Mandukya_Upanishad.pdf (accessed on 26th October 2017)
28. "Children's Conceptions of Dreams", JD Woolley and HM Wellman, *Cognitive Development*, Vol 7, No 3, 1992, pp 365-80.
29. *Freud's World: An Encyclopedia of His Life and Times* by Luis A Cordon, pp 223-5, Greenwood, Santa Barbara, California, 2012.
30. *The Way of Tao: Discourses on Lao Tse's Tao-Te-King*, Part II, Bhagwan Shree Rajneesh, translated by Dolli Didi, p 18, Motilal Banarsidass, Delhi, 1979.

31. *Commentary on the Bhagavadgita* by Swami Krishnananda, pp 45-6, The Divine Life Society, Rishikesh, India. https://www.swami-krishnananda.org/bgita/Commentary_Bhagavadgita.pdf (accessed on 26th October 2017)

32. *The Recollections of Eugene P Wigner: As Told to Andrew Szanton*, Andrew Szanton, p 318, Springer, 1992.

5

Is Future Predictable?

> Everything is determined, the beginning as well as the end, by forces over which we have no control. It is determined for the insect, as well as for the star. Human beings, vegetables, or cosmic dust, we all dance to a mysterious tune, intoned in the distance by an invisible piper.
>
> – *Albert Einstein*

> Whatever this body is to do whatever experiences it is to pass through was already decided.... The only freedom man has is to strive for and acquire the *jnana* which will enable him not to identify himself with the body.
>
> – *Ramana Maharshi*

The past is something which has already happened. It is fixed and unchangeable, but the future is uncertain and unknown. The past evokes nostalgia; the future, hope and excitement. Be it the weather or the movement of the stock exchange or individual fortunes, all of us are interested in knowing the future. It is not surprising therefore that soothsayers and fortune-tellers have always had it easy while playing upon these human frailties. But can the future be predicted? Are things predetermined or do we have free will to change them? Does the future exist in order to get predicted? And if it does not exist, can we predict it? Even if the future does exist, will knowing it not give us the ability to change the very thing we are trying to predict? These are the questions that we shall explore in this chapter.

The efforts to understand natural phenomenon started from the very dawn of the civilization. Thales (625-546 BC) was the first to proclaim that every event had a natural cause and rejected various supernatural, religious or mythological explanations for natural phenomena. Another Greek philosopher, Leucippus proclaimed (5th century BC) that everything was composed entirely of various imperishable, indivisible elements called atoms. In Indian philosophy, Kanada of the Vaisheshika School proposed that all objects were made of indivisible *paramanus* (atoms). Although the exact period in which he lived is not certain, some people contend that he proposed the atomic theory at least a century before Leucippus.

Laws of Motion

In Aristotelian view, the natural state of motion was rest. A force was required to be continuously applied to keep things in motion and this view prevailed until Galileo proved that a force was required to bring change in motion. An object at rest would continue to be at rest and equally one in motion would continue to remain in uniform motion unless acted upon by a force. Galileo was studying the motion of a rolling ball over a wooden inclined plane to establish a mathematical relation between the length of the inclined plane and the time taken by the ball to cover it. From the experiment, he concluded that the ball would reach the bottom of the inclined plane at the same speed if released from the same height, regardless of the inclination of the plane. He further argued that if the ball was then forced to roll up on another inclined plane, it would attain the same height - the height from where it was released. The speed of the ball increased rolling down and decreased rolling up on an inclined plane.

He reasoned, therefore, that it would continue to move with a constant speed on a horizontal surface, if the friction was ignored:

> Furthermore we may remark that any velocity once imparted to a moving body will be rigidly maintained as long as the external causes of acceleration or retardation are removed, a condition which is found only on horizontal planes; for in the case of planes which slope downwards there is already present a cause of acceleration, while on planes sloping upward there is retardation; from this it follows that motion along a horizontal plane is perpetual; for, if the velocity be uniform, it cannot be diminished or slackened, much less destroyed.[1]

Although today it appears to be self-evident, it was a great breakthrough in understanding the nature of motion. Rene Descartes, a French philosopher, mathematician and contemporary of Galileo, independently reached similar conclusions about the nature of motion – that once a body was in motion it would continue to remain so in a straight line. He also prescribed the rules that governed collision between two moving bodies. These ideas were further developed, refined and formalized by Newton into three laws of motion in the famous book *Mathematical Principles of Natural Philosophy* published in 1687. These laws established a relationship between force (cause) and motion (effect) and hence were an attempt to predict future of an object in motion. According to the first law of motion, an object continues to remain in rest or uniform motion unless an external force is applied on it. Imagine a ball moving with a speed of 1 m/s, it will continue to move with the same speed unless we stop it by applying force on it. Had it been otherwise, the ball would have changed its speed on its own, but the future of the ball is sealed. The ball does not possess free will to change its motion.

The second law of motion is even more precisely deterministic and states that if a force is applied on an object, the acceleration caused is proportional to the force. If the force is doubled, the acceleration will also be doubled, essentially meaning that the ball in the above example will come to halt in a predetermined time if a force is applied to it against its motion. The ball has no choice in determining when it will come to rest, that time is fixed. Newton thus led the foundation of scientific determinism by stating that physical objects obey well defined and precise laws and these laws are universal. So, if the initial position and velocity of any object and the forces acting upon it are known, its position and velocity can be calculated at any point of time in the future. And if we can do it for one, the same can be repeated for any number of objects, indeed for the entire universe.

Laplace's Audacity

Science made rapid progress throughout the seventeenth and eighteenth centuries, and what were once attributed to the divine could now be explained by it. As predicted by Edmund Halley, an English astronomer, a comet, which was later named as Halley's Comet, made its appearance in 1758. Although Halley did not live to see his prediction come true, it was a great validation of the law of universal gravitation proposed by Newton. Earlier, the sudden appearance of such objects in the sky was considered a bad omen, a sign of God's opprobrium. Everything now appeared within the grasp of science, and in this optimistic exuberance, Pierre-Simon de Laplace, a French scientist, formulated the doctrine of determinism in 1812:

> We ought then to regard the present state of the universe as the effect of its anterior state and as the cause of the one which is to follow. Given for one instant an intelligence which could comprehend all the forces by which nature is animated and the respective situation of the beings who compose it – an intelligence sufficiently vast to submit these data to analysis – it would embrace in the same formula the

movements of the greatest bodies of the universe and those of the lightest atom; for it, nothing would be uncertain and the future, as the past, would be present to its eyes.[2]

Laplace realized the vastness of the task involved in determining the future of the 'greatest bodies' and the 'lightest atom', and he never speculated whether such an intellect capable of knowing everything could ever exist, but the theoretical possibility of determinism he had little doubt in. Laplace's dreams could be accomplished if we knew all the forces operating in the universe.

We encounter different types of forces in our everyday life: when a ball is thrown up in the air, it gradually slows down, stops and rushes back towards the earth. When a ball is hit by a bat, it changes direction and a rolling ball in a cricket field gradually slows down. The former is caused by gravity, which is a fundamental force, and the latter - both impulse and friction - are non-fundamental forces. These contact forces actually arise from a fundamental force called electromagnetic force. Today we know that there are only four fundamental forces that operate in the universe. The first one is gravitational force which has been dealt with adequately in Chapter 1. It acts on any two masses no matter how far apart they are, which means that it has infinite range. It is responsible for large scale structures in the universe and is the weakest of all fundamental forces. The second is electromagnetic force to which we now turn our attention.

Early Developments in Magnetism and Electricity

It was known since ancient times that a special type of stone called lodestone attracted iron. The compass had also been invented but nobody could explain its functioning. The first systematic study of magnetism was presented by William Gilbert, an English physicist, in his book *De Magnete* (On the Magnet) in the year 1600. The experiments that he conducted were not entirely original and he did borrow ideas from others but he definitely provided a systematic theory of magnetism. He was the first to propose that the earth was a giant magnet and that was why a compass always aligned in a north-south direction. Although he knew that amber when rubbed attracted tiny particles of straw, wood, or metal shavings, he described the 'feeble attraction' of amber as a phenomenon distinct from magnetism, which was a mistake as we will see later. He argued that many substances such as diamond, sapphire, opal, glass etc possess similar attractive power and called them 'electrics' from which the word electricity has been derived.

Almost 150 years after the publication of *De Magnete*, Benjamin Franklin, an American polymath, claimed in the *Pennsylvania Gazette* published on 19th October 1752 to have flown a silk kite fitted with a sharp pointed wire into a thunder gust and received electric shock through the kite's wet cord in the knuckle, establishing that lightning was akin to electricity. This has been the stuff of elementary science textbooks for many years but serious doubt has been cast over his claim in recent times due to several reasons: There was no independent witness to corroborate it; the essential details like the place and the time of the experiment were missing; and neither was this experiment repeated nor demonstrated to any group of people.[3]

Coulomb Discovers the Laws Governing Electric Charges

Charles Augustin Coulomb, a retired French military engineer, designed a torsion balance to measure minute forces – the apparatus was so sensitive that it could measure forces equal to one ten thousandths of a grain. The apparatus consisted of a needle made of a filament of silk covered in Spanish wax suspended by a silver thread from a torsion head. One end of the needle had a pith ball of 4.5-6.8 mm diameter while the other had a disc of paper to balance the needle. A narrow glass tube covered some portion of the silver thread and ended in a wide cylindrical case which housed the needle. The lid of the cylindrical case contained a hole through which another pith ball was lowered into the case in a manner such that the two pith balls touched each other. A small conductor (a pin with a large head) carrying electric charge was brought inside the cylinder though the hole and made to touch one of the balls. The charge residing on the conductor was equally distributed to the balls and therefore the balls repelled each other. As the needle was deflected, the wire got twisted producing torsion force in opposite direction. The two forces - electric repulsion and torsion - became equal when the separation between the two balls was 36 degrees. Coulomb further twisted the suspended wire with the help of a knob fixed in the torsion head. The extra torsion created in the wire could only be balanced by greater force of repulsion between the two balls and therefore they came closer to each other.[4]

From three readings obtained during the experiment conducted in 1785, Coulomb concluded that the force of repulsion between like charges was inversely proportional to the square of the distance between them: if the distance between two charges were halved, the force would become four times. Two years later he performed similar experiment on unlike charges (one positive and one negative) by slightly modifying the apparatus. His conclusion: Unlike charges attracted each other and also followed the inverse square law. Although the Coulomb's famous law is now given by the equation $F = kq_1q_2/r^2$, he never explicitly stated that the magnitude of the force between two charges is proportional to the product of quantity of their charges as it appears in the numerator of the equation.[5] Please recall from Chapter 1 that the gravitational force also follows the inverse square law as $F = Gm_1m_2/r^2$.

Electric Current Produces Magnetism

Thus far only static electricity was known to the world, the likes of which can easily be produced by rubbing a comb with dry hair - we know from personal experience that such a comb attracts small pieces of paper. Coulomb's law laid down the rules of interaction between two static charges, but the first person, who made the charges flow continuously from one place to another, was an Italian physicist, Alessandro Volta. In 1800, Volta built the first electric cell consisting of a series of twenty cups filled with salt water, and in the water were dipped metallic plates, alternately made of silver and zinc. Every plate was connected with the adjacent plate with the help of a metallic arc. He immersed one of his left fingers in the water of the first cup and touched the first arc with the other hand, then the second arc, and so on. He felt the shock while touching the third arc and its strength progressively increased until the last. Volta then placed another series of twenty cups alternately containing zinc and silver plate, reversing the sequence. When he touched successively the 21st, 22nd, 23rd arc and so on, the force of electricity progressively reduced and ultimately disappeared. Every pair of silver-zinc plates acted as a cell and voltage progressively increased when they were connected in series. His body acted as a conductor, which completed the circuit and current began to flow. The next series acted as a set of batteries in reverse direction, gradually bringing the voltage to zero.[6]

Scientists had long suspected that electric and magnetic phenomena were somehow related. The invention of the battery made it possible to conduct experiments to find the link between the two. Some people thought that a current carrying wire would align in north-south direction just like a magnet but it did not prove to be so. In the summer of 1820, a Danish physicist, Hans Christian Oersted was studying the impact of electric current on a magnetic needle. He made a battery consisting of 20 copper troughs, twelve inches in length and height and two and half in breadth. The troughs contained largely water but some sulphuric and nitric acid as well and the electrodes were alternately made of copper and zinc. The opposite ends of the battery were joined by a piece of wire, the straight part of which was placed above a magnetic needle such that the wire was parallel to the needle. When current flowed through the wire, the magnetic needle was deflected by as much as 45 degrees. He then placed the wire below the needle, but again parallel to it, and noticed that the needle was now deflected in the opposite direction. He used wires of different material - gold, silver, platinum, iron etc - but the results were the same. Oersted concluded that a magnetic field was created around the wire and the nature of the magnetic effect was circular because the needle was deflected westward when the wire was kept above it and eastward when kept below.[7]

Magnet Generates Electricity

Oersted established that electric current produced magnetic effect but the reverse that electricity could be generated by a magnet was yet to be demonstrated. This was accomplished by Michael Faraday, son of a poor blacksmith, who hardly had any formal schooling. Although Faraday left school at the age of fourteen to work as an apprentice to a local bookbinder, he was a voracious reader. In 1812, Faraday attended popular lectures given by Humphry Davy at the Royal Institution, which used to attract a large crowd. A year later, he was appointed as a chemical assistant by Davy at the Royal Institution. From then onwards, he never looked back and made several great discoveries in the field of electricity.

In order to generate electricity from a magnet, Faraday wrapped a long copper wire around a wooden cylinder and ensured that two adjacent turns did not touch each other by interposing a thin cord between them. The wire coil was then covered by a layer of muslin, and over it another coil of copper was wound in a similar fashion. Faraday repeated this process until 12 coils were wound around the wooden cylinder, each insulated from the other. The free ends of 2nd, 4th, 6th, 8th, 10th and 12th coils were joined together and similarly odd coils were also connected. The two ends of one coil were connected to a battery. He hoped that the electric current passing through the first coil would produce a magnetic field, which, in turn, would induce current in the second coil. Therefore, he connected the two ends of the second coil to a galvanometer, a device to measure electric current. When he switched on the battery, he did not notice any movement in the galvanometer; therefore, he increased the power of the battery - from ten pairs of plates to a hundred pairs of plates - and the length of the wire from initial 156 feet to 203 feet. Eventually he did notice a small deflection in the galvanometer when the battery was switched on, and also a deflection in the opposite direction when it was switched off. The galvanometer showed no movement when steady electric current was flowing in the first coil.[8]

Maxwell Unites Electricity and Magnetism

Today we know that while an electric current produces magnetic field, only a change in magnetic field induces electric current. That is why when the switch was turned on and off, the electric current was induced in the second coil temporarily as there was a sudden change in magnetic field. Faraday's experiment put a seal of confirmation on the underlying unity between electricity and magnetism but a theoretical framework was still missing. This missing piece of the puzzle was put in place by a Scottish scientist James Clerk Maxwell in the 1860s when he proposed electromagnetic field theory beautifully captured in his 20 general equations. These equations were further simplified into four elegant ones by Oliver Heaviside in 1884, but they are known as Maxwell's equations. Maxwell brought the second grand unification in physics after Newton who had established that the force that pulls an apple towards the earth is the same which keeps the earth in a circular orbit around the sun. Maxwell was also the founder of the Cavendish Laboratory at the University of Cambridge, which played – as we will see shortly – a stellar role in the discovery of the structure of the atom.

The two fundamental forces – gravitation and electromagnetism – have many similarities. They follow inverse square law, which means that the magnitude of force quadruples when the distance between the two objects is halved. Both have infinite range: no matter how far two masses or charges are, they still exert a force, however small, on each other. These two fundamental forces manifest in different ways in our everyday life. When you are standing up on the ground, the gravitational force of the earth pulls you down but an equal and opposite electromagnetic force in upward direction cancels it, in the absence of which you would sink into the ground. When you push open a door, it is the electromagnetic force again that is in operation. Friction, without which we would not be in a position to walk on a surface, is also electromagnetic in nature. All the forces that we encounter in our everyday life are a manifestation of these two fundamental forces.

The remaining two fundamental forces – strong and weak nuclear force – are short range forces, and they operate at subatomic scale. The range of strong nuclear force is $\sim 10^{-15}$ metre, roughly the size of nucleus of an atom, and that of weak nuclear force is $\sim 10^{-18}$ metre only. Since they work at microscopic scale, we never feel them directly in the macroscopic world, but they are very important because without them, the atoms would not hold together, and consequently the material world in which we live would not exist. To understand these forces, therefore, we begin by looking at the structure of the atoms.

Discovery of Electrons

Atoms were thought to be the smallest constituents of matter since ancient times but the empirical evidence of this was provided for the first time by an English chemist, John Dalton, in the early nineteenth century. He observed that when two elements combined with each other in different proportion to form more than one compound, the weights of one element that combined with a fixed weight of the other were in a ratio of small whole numbers. This can be explained by a simple example: 1 gram of hydrogen combine with 8 gram of oxygen to form water and with 16 gram of oxygen to form hydrogen peroxide. The ratio of weight of oxygen that combines with 1 gram of hydrogen is 16/8, which is 2, a simple whole number. Dalton argued that it was possible only if the smallest constituents of matter combined in discrete ratios. If A and B were two elements, different compounds could be formed by their atoms in following ways: $A + B = AB$ (one atom of A and one atom of B), $2A + B = A_2B$, $A + 2B = AB_2$ etc. A lecture that he delivered on January 30, 1810 at the Royal Institution captures the crux of his idea beautifully: "Matter, though divisible in an extreme degree, is nevertheless not infinitely divisible ... there must be some point beyond which we cannot go in the division of matter. The existence of these ultimate particles of matter can scarcely be doubted, though they are probably much too small ever to be exhibited by microscopic improvements."[9]

Dalton's model of indivisible atoms was consigned to history after electrons were discovered in 1897 by JJ Thomson – the third Cavendish Professor of Experimental Physics at Cambridge after Maxwell and Lord Rayleigh – while studying the discharge of electricity through gases at low pressure. Such experiments had begun as early as 1838 when Faraday used a crude vacuum pump to reduce pressure within a glass tube. A number of scientists in coming decades repeated the experiment several times with more sophisticated vacuum pumps capable of creating up to one millionth of the atmospheric pressure. The basic apparatus consisted of a hollow glass tube from which air was sucked out. The inside of the tube was fitted with two metal plates, which were connected to the two ends of a battery – the metal plate connected to the negative terminal of the battery was called cathode and the one to the positive terminal, anode. When the battery was switched on, a glow appeared in the region between the two plates. As the pressure was further reduced, the glow shifted towards the anode end – something was travelling from cathode to anode. The glow was also found to be deflected by magnetic field, which indicated that they were a stream of negatively charged particles. (A charge moving in a magnetic field experiences a force and the direction of movement of the particle depends on whether it is positively or negatively charged, keeping other things constant). On the other hand, when the glow was directed on a gold foil, they emerged from the other side in a diffused form. Since no particles had been observed to pass through a metal, it was fair to conclude that it was some sort of radiation (light).

The Germans, led by Heinrich Hertz, argued that the glow was a wave because, besides penetrating metals, it was not deflected by an electric field. Had they been a stream of negative charges, they should have been deflected towards the positive end of the applied electric field. The English, William Crookes being chief amongst them, insisted that the rays consisted of particles because the radiation was not affected by a magnetic field. The stalemate continued until 1997 when Thomson successfully demonstrated that cathode rays were indeed deflected by the electric field. He allowed the cathode rays to pass through a slit in the anode. This was done to make the beam narrow in order to study its deflection more accurately. The rays then travelled between two parallel aluminium plates about 5 cm long and at a distance of 1.5 cm apart and fell on the right end of the tube, which had fluorescent coating. The point at which the rays hit the spherical tube glowed brightly, which enabled Thomson to measure the deflection.[10] His observations are worth quoting:

> At high exhaustions [very low pressure] the rays were deflected when the two aluminium plates were connected with the terminals of a battery of small storage cells; the rays were depressed when the upper plate was connected with the negative pole of the battery, the lower with the positive, and raised when the upper plate was connected with the positive, the lower with the negative pole. The deflexion was proportional to the difference of potential between the plates, and I could detect the deflexion when the potential difference was as small as two volts. It was only when **the vacuum was a good one that the deflexion took place** [emphasis added]....[11]

Why did Thomson succeed where Hertz had failed? In Hertz's experiment, enough gas was still left in the tube, and when an electric field was applied perpendicular to the motion of the rays, it was ionised. The positive ions moved down towards negative plate and the electrons moved up towards the positive plate. This created an electric field in reverse direction and neutralised the electric field applied by Hertz. (These electrons should not be confused with the stream electrons that emanated from the cathode at the left end of the tube and were rushing towards the right end. They were produced in the local region where the electric field was applied perpendicular to the motion of the electrons.) Since the electric field was neutralised, the rays passed the region without any deflection. Thomson produced a better vacuum, leaving hardly any gas in the tube, which could be ionised. Thomson experimented with different gases - air, hydrogen and carbonic acid - and with cathodes made of aluminium and platinum, but the results were the same. Therefore, he concluded:

> As the cathode rays carry a charge of negative electricity, are deflected by an electrostatic force as if they were negatively electrified, and are acted on by a magnetic force in just the way in which this force would act on a negatively electrified body moving along the path of these rays, I can see no escape from the conclusion that they are charges of negative electricity carried by particles of matter. The question[s] next arise: What are these particles? Are they atoms, or molecules, or matter in a still finer state of subdivision?[12]

To answer these questions, he first measured the speed of these rays by subjecting them simultaneously to electric as well as magnetic field in a manner that the deflection caused by the one was neutralised by the other field. The speed so calculated turned out to be much less than that of light, which strengthened his argument against Hertz. If these rays were radiation, they would travel with the speed of light. He then calculated the mass/charge ratio of the particles from the angle of deviation of the rays, the strength of electric and magnetic field and the length of aluminium plates (5 cm). This ratio was one thousandth of mass/charge ratio of hydrogen ion obtained during electrolysis of water. Thomson argued that this could be either due to smallness of mass or bigness of charge of the particles. He relied on Philipp Lenard's observation that cathode rays on an average travelled a far greater distance before colliding with the molecules in the air than air molecules themselves. This could be possible only if the particles in cathode rays were much smaller than ordinary molecules.[10]

Since the particles coming from the cathode were smaller than atoms, argued Thomson, they must be constituents of atoms. Clearly, atoms were not indivisible but consisted of particles that he called 'corpuscles', later named electrons. But this posed a problem: if atoms consisted of negatively charged electrons, how could atoms be electrically neutral? Some part of atoms must carry equal positive charge to cancel the negative charge of electrons. Therefore, he imagined the atom as a spherical ball of uniform positive charge while the electrons were not only embedded in the sphere but also moved in circular orbits. In his model, the mass of atom was contained in the electrons and not in the positive sphere. This implied that an atom was made of thousands of electrons, but his own research a little later showed that the number of electrons was only of the order of atomic mass and not in thousands as he had predicted. The model faded into oblivion sooner rather than later and was replaced by Rutherford's. His electron, however, has withstood time and continues to remain one of the elementary particles, which cannot be subdivided further.

Atom has a Lot of Empty Space

Ernest Rutherford had discovered alpha particles in 1899 when he was working in McGill University in Montreal. At that time, it was not known that alpha particles were actually helium atoms, stripped of their electrons, that is, helium nucleus. Rutherford, however, knew that alpha particle had positive charge by observing its deflection by electric and magnetic field, much in the same manner Thomson had discovered electrons. He also found that e/m (charge/mass ratio) of the particle was 5,070, approximately half of the value of hydrogen ion. If the alpha particle carried unit positive charge its mass would be twice that of the hydrogen atom. Alternatively, if the particle had two units of positive charge, its mass would nearly equal that of the atom of helium. Rutherford was more inclined to believe the latter, but he wanted to verify it by accurately measuring the charge of an individual alpha particle.

In 1907, he returned to Britain and assumed the Chair of Physics at the Victoria University, Manchester. Here, with the help of Hans Geiger, his research student, he attempted to accurately measure the charge of an individual alpha particle. Since each alpha particle falling on a screen of phosphorescent zinc sulphide was known to produce a visible scintillation, Rutherford proposed to count the number of scintillations with the aid of a microscope, calculate the total charge of all particles, and then divide it by the number of particles to obtain the charge of one particle. It was during such experiments in 1908 that Geiger noticed significant scattering of alpha particles during their passage through matter. The apparatus consisted of a glass tube two metres in length and two centimetres in radius. A source of alpha particles was kept inside the tube towards the left end. They passed through a slit of 0.9 mm and fell on a zinc sulphide screen cemented at the right end of the tube. A geometrical image of the slit about 2 mm in breadth was formed on the screen.[13] This was expected because the particles travelled unhindered through the vacuum in a straight line and fell on the screen at the right, but when the slit was covered with gold foil, Geiger noticed considerable scattering of the particles:

> In a good vacuum, hardly any scintillations were observed outside of the geometrical image of the slit. But on allowing a little air into the tube, the area where scintillations were observed greatly increased. By moving the microscope along the whole screen and counting the number of scintillations at definite intervals, usually every second millimetre, a curve of the distribution of the alpha particles was obtained. The number of scintillations was small at the extreme boundary of the screen but rapidly increased towards the centre of the beam. Similar results were obtained in a vacuum, if the slit were covered with leaves of gold or aluminium.[14]

Geiger continued the experiment with some modifications in the apparatus over the next five years. He varied the speed of alpha particles and thickness of the material, and also used different materials (gold, platinum, tin etc). The results were startling: although most alpha particles just passed through the gold foil without any deviation, 1 in 8,000 showed deflections by 90 degree or more, that is, they almost turned back into the direction from which they were fired.[15] These observations puzzled Rutherford as such large deviations could not be accounted for by Thomson's model, in which positive charge was uniformly distributed over the entire volume of the atom, and therefore, the alpha particles should have just passed though the gold foil without any appreciable deviation. Rutherford, therefore, proposed in a paper written in 1911 that almost the entire mass and positive charge were concentrated at the centre of the atom, called nucleus, and much of the space inside an atom was empty. The alpha particles that came very close to the nuclei of gold atoms were repulsed (like charges repel each other) according to Coulomb's law.[16]

Imagine a large and rectangular but thin sheet of metal of uniform thickness kept in front of a firing squad. The squad is then asked to fire randomly in the direction of the sheet. The bullets hit the sheet, create holes and pass through it without any difficulty. The sheet is now melted and recast into a wire mesh in a manner that almost all the mass is concentrated at the intersections of the mesh, thick enough to resist a bullet. When the bullets are fired at the mesh, most of them pass through the empty region of the mesh, but some hit the intersections and get deflected. The bullets are alpha particles and the sheet and the mesh represent the structure of atoms in the gold foil experiment according to Thomson and Rutherford respectively.

Genius of Bohr

Readers may be curious to know how Rutherford arranged the electrons in an atom. He was inclined to the idea, put forward by a Japanese physicist, Hantaro Nagaoka, in which the positive nucleus attracted the electrons carrying negative charge by an electrostatic force that kept them locked in circular orbits, much in the same way the planets revolved around the sun. The trouble with this model was that it was inherently unstable because although the electrons were moving in orbits at constant speed, they underwent change in the direction of the motion, and hence acceleration. And the laws of classical electrodynamics dictated that the accelerating electrons should be constantly emitting radiation, losing energy and spiralling into the nucleus.

A young Danish physicist, Niels Bohr, arrived in Cambridge in September 1911 to work with Thomson in the same year in which Rutherford had published his paper on the structure of the atom. He was soon disappointed as Thomson showed little interest in his work. Fortunately, he had a chance meeting with Rutherford during a visit to Manchester, who invited young Bohr to work with him, a proposal he readily accepted. Bohr stayed in Manchester from March to July 1912 before returning to Copenhagen, and it was here that he got interested in the apparent instability of Rutherford's model.[17] Bohr realised that reliance on classical electrodynamics would not resolve the problem in Rutherford's model and the clue to the behaviour of electrons could be found in the hypothesis proposed by Planck in 1900 that electromagnetic radiation was emitted in packets, that is, discrete quanta. Planck's hypothesis was affirmed by photoelectric effect of Einstein, as we have seen in the previous chapter. Moreover, Bohr knew from the work of other scientists that the spectrum of hydrogen was composed of discrete wavelengths.

In order to fully appreciate the arguments of Bohr, we need to understand the spectrum of the hydrogen atom. Recall the gas tube experiments conducted by scientists that led to the discovery of electrons. When a small quantity of gas was present in the tube, the whole of the tube was filled with a glow of light. Scientists succeeded in discovering electrons only after the pressure in the tube was considerably reduced, which allowed the passage of electrons unhindered. In similar experiments, when scientists passed the light emitted from a tube containing a small amount of hydrogen gas through a prism, they found that the light was composed of four specific wavelengths: 410, 434, 486 and 656 nanometre. In contrast, normal white light coming from the sun consisted of all wavelengths between 380 and 740 nanometre. The spectrum of white light was continuous but that of hydrogen was discrete. This was perplexing: why should hydrogen atoms emit light of certain specific wavelengths?

These observations had been in the scientific domain since the 1880s, but nobody was ready to take the giant leap - Bohr seized it. He postulated, in a paper published in 1913, that electrons could move around the nucleus in certain specific orbits of fixed radii, and when they revolved in those orbits, they defied the law of classical electrodynamics, that is, they did not radiate energy. Each allowed orbit had a specific energy level and an electron could only jump from a higher orbit to a lower orbit by emitting light of a specific wavelength equal to energy difference between two orbits. Alternatively, it could absorb light of a given wavelength and move to a higher orbit. In case of a hydrogen atom, an electron revolved around the nucleus carrying one proton. When an electric current was passed through hydrogen gas at low pressure, the atoms were excited and the electrons jumped from orbit 1 to orbit 2 or 3 etc. When they fell back into the lower orbits, light of specific wavelengths was emitted. Bohr argued that had this not been the case, the spectrum of light emitted from hydrogen atoms would have been continuous, comprising of all wavelengths. The predictions of Bohr's model with respect to emission lines of hydrogen spectrum also matched the experimental observations, giving credence to the model.

Missing Particle is Finally Located

The Rutherford-Bohr model was not complete because neutrons were yet to be discovered. Readers might be wondering as to how the model took into account the absence of neutrons. This can be illustrated with an example: a carbon atom, we now know, has six protons and six neutrons in its nucleus, and therefore its mass is 12 units. The positive charge of six units in the nucleus is balanced by six negatively charged electrons, which revolve around the nucleus. In Rutherford-Bohr model, the carbon atom could possess a mass of 12 units only by assuming that its nucleus comprised of 12 protons. However, it was known that the carbon atom contained only six electrons, which left an excess charge of six units. Therefore, it was hypothesised that the nucleus of a carbon atom also contained six electrons to neutralise the excess charge, but there was no clarity on how exactly these electrons arranged themselves inside the nucleus. Though Rutherford proposed 'electrons within nucleus' model, he did not dismiss the possibility of the existence of a neutral particle[18], and such a particle was indeed discovered later.

James Chadwick was a student of Rutherford at Manchester, and later he went to study beta radiation under Geiger in Berlin. When World War I broke out, he was interned at a racetrack in Ruhleben, Berlin. The War ended in 1919 and young Chadwick soon joined Rutherford, who had become Cavendish Professor at Cambridge. There he continued his research on the structure of atoms under the guidance of Rutherford. Meanwhile, the evidence of the existence of a neutral particle had been growing throughout the 1920s, but it was hard to detect it because it had no charge, and therefore could not be deflected either by an electric field or a magnetic field. Ultimately, Chadwick discovered a particle with zero charge and mass slightly higher than the mass of a proton in 1932, which was called neutron.* The men, who unravelled the structure of the atom, Thomson, Rutherford, Bohr and Chadwick, all had some association with the Cavendish Laboratory established by Maxwell.

Strong Nuclear Force Holds the Nucleus

So long as the nucleus of the atom was thought to be made up of protons and electrons, it could be argued - even if unconvincingly - that the repulsion between protons was somehow balanced by the attraction between protons and electrons. But the discovery of neutrons raised a serious doubt on the stability of the nucleus. Recall that the Coulomb's force between two charges is inversely proportional to the square of the distance between them. If the distance between them is halved, the force becomes four times stronger. Therefore, the repulsive force between protons confined within a very small nucleus would be so enormous - the gravitational attractive force between them would be too feeble (weaker by one trillion trillion trillion times) to resist the Coulomb's repulsion - that it would be ripped apart. Clearly, there was something which held the nucleus together, and this led Eugene Wigner, a Hungarian-American Physicist, to propose that when protons and neutrons were close - within a range of one million billionth of a metre - to one another, they felt a strong attractive force called the strong nuclear force. If this force acted like gravity over infinite range, all protons and neutrons would coalesce into a single nucleus, and the universe, as we know, would not exist.

Weak Nuclear Force Explains Beta Decay

This brings us to the fourth fundamental force, which, like the strong force, was discovered while trying to make sense

---

*The details of Chadwick's experiment have been deliberately omitted because of the complexity involved in interpreting its results. Readers can refer to advanced texts for this purpose.

of the phenomenon that had defied the scientists for long. When Rutherford was studying radiation emanating from uranium, he had noticed two different types of radiation: alpha and beta. While the alpha radiation was easily absorbed by a thin aluminium foil, the beta radiation was more penetrative in character. The alpha radiation later turned out to be particles of mass of 4 units and positive charge of 2 units and beta radiation was found to be actually a stream of electrons. Further experiments revealed that while the alpha particles were ejected with discrete values of energy, the electrons (beta particles) possessed all possible values of energy from zero to an upper limit. The emission of electrons from the nucleus also violated the law of conservation of energy - the energy with which the electron was emitted was less than the energy lost by the nucleus. In 1930, Wolfgang Pauli, a Swiss and American physicist, hinted at the existence of a hitherto unknown particle, which might have carried the missing energy away.

The particle was later called neutrino by Enrico Fermi, an Italian physicist, but it was not discovered until 1956. Today we know that beta decay is a process in which either a neutron decays into a proton by emitting an electron plus an antineutrino or a proton decays into a neutron by emitting an antielectron and a neutrino. The force that is responsible for beta decay of neutrons and protons is the weak nuclear force, its range is shorter than the strong nuclear force and it is the weakest force after gravitation.

Laplace Faces Obstacles

Scientists dream of uniting these four fundamental forces into one force, called the Theory of Everything, which can explain all phenomena in the universe. In fact, they have succeeded in demonstrating that at very high level of energy electromagnetic force and weak nuclear force coalesce into a single force called electroweak force. Assume that such a hypothetical force has been discovered and is expressed by a set of beautiful equations. If these equations were to be given to Laplace with a hypothetical supercomputer capable of storing and processing the initial values of all variables, would he then be able to predict everything in the universe, to its minutest details.

Maxwell struck a note of caution that even if all the forces acting on a system were fully known, it would be difficult to predict the future because its initial states could only be known approximately, and in an unstable system, a very small error in the initial measurement could lead to a large variation over time:

> When the state of things is such that an infinitely small variation of the present state will alter only by an infinitely small quantity the state at some future time, the condition of the system, whether at rest or in motion, is said to be stable; but when an infinitely small variation in the present state may bring about a finite difference in the state of the system in a finite time, the condition of the system is said to be unstable. It is manifest that the existence of unstable conditions renders impossible the prediction of future events, if our knowledge of the present state is only approximate, and not accurate.[19]

Laplace's notion of hard determinism came under further criticism from a fellow French mathematician, Henri Poincare, who amplified the arguments given by Maxwell:

> If a cone is balanced on its point, we know very well that it will fall, but we do not know to which side; it seems that chance alone will decide. If the cone were perfectly symmetrical, if its axis were perfectly vertical, if it were subject to no other force but gravity, it would not fall at all. But the slightest defect of symmetry will make it lean slightly to one side or other, and as soon as it leans, be it ever so little, it will fall altogether to that side. Even if the symmetry is perfect, a very slight trepidation, or a breath of air, may make

> it incline a few seconds of arc, and that will be enough to determine its fall and even the direction of its fall, which will be that of the original inclination.[20]

Poincare illustrated the difficulties in predicting weather due to unstable nature of such systems:

> Why have meteorologists such difficulty in predicting the weather with any certainty? Why is it that showers and even storms seem to come by chance, so that many people think it quite natural to pray for rain or fine weather, though they would consider it ridiculous to ask for an eclipse by prayer? We see that great disturbances are generally produced in regions where the atmosphere is in unstable equilibrium. The meteorologists see very well that the equilibrium is unstable, that a cyclone will be formed somewhere, but exactly where they are not in a position to say; a tenth of a degree more or less at any given point, and the cyclone will burst here and not there, and extend its ravages over districts it would otherwise have spared. If they had been aware of this tenth of a degree, they could have known it beforehand, but the observations were neither sufficiently comprehensive nor sufficiently precise, and that is the reason why it all seems due to intervention of chance.[21]

The wave-particle duality of Louis de Broglie, another Frenchman and a physicist, posed a more serious threat to Laplace's determinism. His hypothesis that the essential nature of matter was dualistic, that is, the matter behaved both like wave and particle, put a more fundamental limitation on predictability. Only three years later, Werner Heisenberg presented his famous uncertainty principle which stated that if we attempted to determine the position of a particle more accurately, our measurement of its speed would be less precise, and vice versa. Although Laplace was also concerned about approximation in the measurement of the initial conditions, his concern probably arose from the inadequacy of measuring instruments. Heisenberg's genius lay in claiming that much like the theoretical limit placed on the speed of any object in Einstein's special theory of relativity, there was a limit with which we could measure two related parameters like, position and speed, time and energy etc. The uncertainty principle emanates from inherent nature of systems and not from inadequacy of measuring instruments.

How Much 'Free Will' Do We Have?

Some might argue philosophically that the idea of predicting future is a contradiction in terms. If I know that I will die tomorrow in a road accident, I will confine myself in a house to defeat the prediction. Ironically, the predictability itself sows the seed of its negation because I have free will to change the course of future. Let us take an example: NASA's Skylab was the first American space station. It was expected that Skylab would stay in space for at least eight years. However, extra solar activity warmed the Earth's outer atmosphere and increased drag on the spacecraft and, in the fall of 1977, scientists determined that Skylab was no longer in a stable orbit. In the weeks leading up to Skylab's fall, NASA made small adjustments to Skylab's position, in an attempt to minimize the odds of the craft disintegrating over a populated area. Fortunately, when Skylab entered the atmosphere and disintegrated on July 11, 1979, the debris fell over the Indian Ocean and a sparsely populated area of Western Australia. The knowledge of Skylab's fall enabled the scientists to interfere in its trajectory to minimize the damage, if altogether not eliminate it. It can still be argued that despite human intervention Skylab did fall and could not be rescued, but it cannot be denied that predictability of an event does create scope for influencing the predicted event.

However, this may not always be true. We know the timings of solar and lunar eclipses with accuracy of seconds, but can we stop or delay this event? Theoretically, it can be argued that if the speed of moon or earth is altered, then the prediction can be failed, but the gravitational force of attraction between the earth and the moon is approximately 2×10^{20} N, the speed of moon is 3,680 km per hour and its kinetic energy is of the order of 10^{28} joule. Any alteration in the speed of moon will require a force of comparative strength and the energy of the order of 10^{28} joule. The largest hydrogen bomb manufactured by mankind can release energy of 4×10^{17} joule, which means that 25 billion such hydrogen bombs will be required to produce the equivalent amount of energy capable of altering the speed of the moon.

A ball falling towards the earth and the motion of the moon orbiting the earth, both are governed by the universal force of gravitation, yet the falling of the ball can be arrested but the revolution of the moon around the earth cannot be stopped because our free will is not unfettered, rather it is constrained by the larger structure of the universe.

The question arises: how much free will do we have? Let us assume that a person is driving the fastest ever vehicle designed by human beings, which moves with a speed of say 10,000 km per hour. The person moves from point A and stops after one hour. He can exercise his free will to be anywhere within a radius of 10,000 km from point A, but not beyond it. Occasionally, human beings are able to stretch this limit, ironically by exercising free will in designing faster vehicles but nonetheless the limit remains. Obviously, we cannot exercise our free will to stop the expansion of the universe.

Imagine a hollow hemispherical bowl, inside which a ball is rolled from the top edge. As the ball moves towards the bottom of the hemisphere, its speed increases till it hits the bottom, and then it rises up with decreasing speed, only to come to rest momentarily at the top edge. The ball can never escape from the hemisphere because it does not possess enough energy to surmount the barrier. No matter how many times the ball is rolled, it is absurd to think that the ball will ever fall off from the bowl. However, at microscopic level such phenomena happen defying the classical laws of physics. Sub-atomic particles like alpha particles, neutron and proton leak out from the nuclei of atoms despite not possessing enough energy to cross the energy barrier. According to the quantum theory, such phenomena have tiny but definite probability of occurrence but it is impossible to predict when a given atom will decay. The decay of the atoms happens randomly. Therefore, at very small scale, the matter displays non-deterministic properties, as if the sub-atomic particles have free will of their own.

Therefore, I shall argue that much like a light beam, which at times behaves like a bunch of particles and at times like a wave, the nature of future is dualistic. I can with great confidence say that a person born in AD 2010 will not be alive in AD 2210. I can almost predict that the person will have died by AD 2140, but what will he be doing at 9:00 AM on the 25th March 2050, it is impossible to tell. What will he be doing at that instant - eating or sleeping or doing nothing depends on what he will choose to do at that point of time. More complicatedly, his 'free will' is not totally free as it depends on a complex interplay of several 'free wills' of people who are in some way related to him. Therefore, the universe is deterministic at a very large scale but non-deterministic at a very small scale. Between these two extremes, determinism and free will coexist. Free will operates within the constraints set by determinism and the limits imposed by determinism are stretched by the operation of free will.

Predicting Human Behaviour and Actions

If the inanimate world is hard to predict, it is harder to predict human behaviour and actions. In behavioural sciences it is well-nigh impossible to perform controlled experiments. If the effect of literacy on birth rate has to be studied, there is no way that the experiment can be repeated while keeping all other variables constant, say for example, the availability of contraceptives or family income. Two phenomena may be correlated but causality between the two is difficult to establish. Worst, the underlying cause of both the phenomena could be a third variable, what is called the 'omitted variable bias' in scientific parlance. Meteorologists at least know the factors affecting the weather and the mathematical equations governing them, but behavioural scientists are much less certain of the factors that affect the outcome, let alone the precise relationship with them. In that sense the prediction of socio-economic phenomena faces a more fundamental obstacle.

Karma and Bondage

Destiny and free will have exercised the minds of philosophers no less than that of the scientists. Religions have struggled equally to reconcile providence with free will. If God decides everything, man is saved from any moral culpability, but morality has been one of the cornerstones of every religion. One attempt to reconcile the two has been to grant the power of foreknowledge to God while man is left free to take actions, but even the foreknowledge restricts the freedom available to man in that he cannot act otherwise than is already known. While every religion has grappled with this dilemma, Hinduism, with its twin belief in *karma* and *reincarnation*, has attempted the most sophisticated explanation of it.

The word *karma* comes from Sanskrit word 'kri', it means 'to do'. *Karma* literally means deed or act. *Karma* means not only action, but also the result of an action. The consequence of an action is a part of the action, and cannot be separated from it. Every action produces its own consequences. The law of *karma* is universal and nobody can escape the consequences of his *karma*; not even Gods. Hindus also believe that the soul is indestructible and it transmigrates from one body to another. The *Bhagavad Gita* states: "Never was there a time when I did not exist, nor you, nor all these kings; nor in the future shall any of us cease to be. As the embodied soul continuously passes, in this body, from boyhood to youth to old age, the soul similarly passes into another body at death. A sober person is not bewildered by such a change."[22] The cycle of life and death can be broken only by attaining *moksha* (liberation), which has been the highest spiritual goal of Hindus.

If *karma* is inescapable then the obvious conclusion that can be drawn is that the future is predetermined because of our past actions and we are merely puppets in the hands of destiny. Therefore, Hindu philosophy has often been accused - and not unreasonably - of being fatalistic in outlook. In its simplest form the *Karmic* theory appears to be purely deterministic, much like the hard determinism in science propagated by Laplace, but the theory of *karma* is subtle and complex and it reconciles determinism with free will.

Karma can be further classified into three categories. *Sanchita karma* is accumulated consequences of actions in present and past lives. Accumulated *karma* does not fructify at once, rather it does at different times, and when it bears fruit, at that moment it becomes *prarabdha karma* - it is that part of *sanchita karma* whose consequences are being manifest at present. The actions that are being performed at present are called *kriyamana karma,* which will bear fruit in the future. Nobody knows when the consequences of an action will manifest. The *karmas* are accumulated from one life to another and it is in this *karmic* cycle that the soul is trapped. So long as there is *karmic* burden, the soul will transmigrate from one body to another. *Karma* can be visualised as a water tank with an inlet and an outlet. The inlet is *kriyamana karma,* the outlet represents *prarabdha karma* and the tank holds *sanchita karma*. The present actions continuously replenish the tank while the enjoyment of fruits or suffering of consequences empties it. We are constrained by our past actions, but within those constraints we are free to make our own future. Nobody has explained this better than the Great Master Ramana Maharshi:

> Neither is everything predestined, nor do we have free will in everything. There was a time when we had free will. We could act as we pleased. We acted, and that act produced a certain result. That "result" became our destiny. We could not escape it. We acted again. This time our free will carried with it the experience of our first act, and was qualified and limited to that extent. This act again produced results, and these results again curtailed our original freedom. Now that we have been acting and producing results for millions of ages, these actions and their reactions act upon us as our unavoidable fate. Our body, mind, intellect, and reasoning are fashioned by these and make us choose a certain course. Our previous acts determine our present life, and our present acts go to make our future. We reap now what we have sown in our previous births, and we shall reap in the future what we are sowing now.[23]

We are free to become anything, a soldier, or a sailor, or a teacher etc., but having chosen a profession, we must abide by its rules, and cannot complain about the restrictions that are put upon us because of that. We can choose to live anywhere in the world, but once we exercise a choice, we will have to suffer the good and the bad of that place. We forego that part of freedom. We are free to act, we act and the act diminishes our free will.

A man came and insulted Buddha but he remained quiet. He listened to the man patiently and thanked him. The man asked surprisingly as to why he was being nice even after getting insulted. Buddha told the man that he had insulted him in the past and been waiting for him to close the account. Now he was free because he had enjoyed the result of his action, otherwise he might have to wait for the next life to settle the account.[24]

If a force is applied on an object, it can resist only up to a limit, but once a threshold is crossed, it has no choice but to move. The object cannot defy the laws of motion. The four fundamental forces apply everywhere in the universe and there is not a single moment when they cease to operate. In the same way the wheel of *karma* moves ceaselessly. "... men are governed by His law, the law of *karma*, which rules the world. God created His law and left the world to its governance, reserving to Himself no right to interfere with its operation."[25]

How does one liberate oneself from the endless cycle of action and result if every act becomes bondage? The *Bhagavad Gita* says it is not action but attachment to the action which creates bondage. Therefore, action should be performed without coveting the result, that is, *nishkama karma*; action without desire. If there is no attachment to the fruits of action, there is no bondage. The bondage is the creation of the ego: One must suffer the consequences of one's action because one falsely takes credit for doing it. The ego is an illusion (*maya*), and if it dissolves, the liberation from the endless cycle of birth and death is certain.

We do not have freedom to travel to another planet as yet because of several difficulties in designing a vehicle that is fast enough, but we may do so in future. The limit of free will can be stretched. Similarly, the law of *karma* restricts our free will, but consciousness can be expanded to break the bond of *karma*. Science and philosophy are two very different disciplines but both are in search of truth – and surprisingly both reach similar conclusions.

If there were no law in the universe, everything would happen randomly, and it would not be possible to make any predictions at all. But there is a rhythm, a design and regularity in the universe. Days follow nights and nights follow days.

Seasons do not change abruptly. The planets do not fly away or into the sun. And because the universe is governed by fixed laws, we are able to make some predictions despite the limitations imposed by the chaotic nature of some systems, our inability to precisely measure the initial conditions and the operation of free will. The question is that if there were no laws, could human beings exist, could any form of life exist and could galaxies, star and planets develop? And the answer is no. Therefore, the universe could not be purely non-deterministic.

Now imagine living in a universe which is absolutely deterministic. Our future would be laid bare down to every detail. We would know whom we would marry, how many children we would have, where we would work and so on. All that gives us happiness, sorrow, excitement and disappointment would be known in advance. There would be no freedom to act differently and life would run like a pre-programmed machine. Human beings would have no moral agency and we would be merely mute spectators to the unfolding events. It would be a terribly boring and frustrating place. Life is beautiful because it has both - design and freedom. We cannot survive without design but we cannot live without freedom.

Notes and References

1. *Dialogue Concerning Two New Sciences by Galileo Galilei*, translated by Henry Crew and Alfonso de Salvio, p 215, Cosimo Classics, New York, 2010.
2. *A Philosophical Essay on Probabilities* by Marquis de Laplace Pierre-Simon, p 4, translated by FW Truscott and FL Emory, Cosimo Classics, New York, 2007.
3. *Bolt of Fate: Benjamin Franklin and His Electric Kite Hoax* by Tom Tucker, pp 135-56, Public Affairs, New York, 2003.
4. *The Pendulum: A Case Study in Physics* by Gregory L Baker and James A Blackburn, pp 99-104, Oxford University Press, 2005.
5. *Ibid*, p 104.

6. "On the Electricity Excited by the Mere Contact of Conducting Substances of Different Kinds", Alessandro Volta, *Philosophical Magazine,* London, Vol 7, No 28, 1800, pp 289-311.
7. "Experiments on the Effect of a Current of Electricity on the Magnetic Needle", HC Oersted, *Annals of Philosophy,* Volume 16, No 94, 1820, pp 273-6.
8. "Experimental Researches in Electricity", Michael Faraday, *Philosophical Transactions* of the Royal Society of London, Volume 122, No 122, 1832, pp 125-62.
9. As quoted in *The Study of Chemical Composition: An Account of its Method and Historical Development* by Ida Freund, p 288, Cambridge University Press, 2014.
10. "Cathode Rays", JJ Thomson, *Philosophical Magazine and Journal of Science,* Vol 44, No 269, 1897, pp 293-316.
11. *Ibid,* p 297.
12. *Ibid,* p 302.
13. "On the Scattering of the α-Particles by Matter", H Geiger, *Proceedings of the Royal Society of London A,* Vol 81, No 546, 1908, pp 174-7.
14. *Ibid,* p 175.
15. "On a Diffuse Reflection of the α-Particles", Hans Geiger and Ernest Marsden, *Proceedings of the Royal Society of London A,* Vol 82, No 557, 1909, pp 495-500.
16. "The Scattering of α and β Particles by Matter and the Structure of the Atom", Ernest Rutherford, *Philosophical Magazine,* Vol 21, No 125, 1911, pp 669-88.
17. *Niels Bohr and the Quantum Atom* by Helge Kragh, pp 44-7, Oxford University Press, 2012.
18. "Bakerian Lecture: Nuclear Constitution of Atoms", Ernest Rutherford, *Proceedings of the Royal Society of London A,* Vol 97, No 686, 1920, pp 374-400.
19. *The Life of James Clerk Maxwell: With a Selection from His Correspondence and Occasional Writings and a Sketch of His Contributions to Science* by Lewis Campbell and William Garnett, p 440, Cambridge University Press, 2010.
20. *Science and Method by Henri Poincare,* translated by Francis Maitland, p 67, Dover Publications, Inc, New York, 2003.
21. *Ibid,* pp 68-9.
22. *Bhagavad Gita As It Is* by AC Bhaktivedanta Swami Prabhupada,

pp 81-3, Bhaktivedanta Book Trust International, Inc, USA, 1989.

23. As quoted in "Free Will, Karma, Reincarnation, Effort, and Grace" by Ramananda Prasad. http://www.gita-society.com/bhagavad-gita-section4/4_Free will.htm (accessed on 21st October 2017)
24. *Secrets of Yoga by Osho*, edited by Prem Chinmaya and Bodhitaru, pp 7-8, Penguin Books, India, 2004.
25. *The Bhagavad Gita: According to Mahatma Gandhi*, p 121, Orient Publishing, New Delhi, 2016.

6

On the Razor's Edge – Why is Balance Essential in Life?

> To light a candle is to cast a shadow. – *Ursula K Le Guin*
>
> Astronomy leads us to a unique event, a universe which was created out of nothing, one with the very delicate balance needed to provide exactly the conditions required to permit life, and one which has an underlying (one might say 'supernatural') plan. – *Arno Penzias*

At every turn after birth, the universe could have taken several possible paths in its journey, and choices were indeed exercised on every turn, but miraculously in a manner that the universe appears to be so exquisitely fashioned as to enable an intelligent species like human beings to emerge. It appears to be a perfect composition of music that cannot withstand even the slightest displacement of a note. It can be argued that these choices turned out to be right by sheer coincidence, and not design, although the probability of occurrence of a series of favourable events would be extremely rare. Imagine that you have won the lottery every year, for the last fifty years. When we roll a dice, the probability of getting any number, say 3, is 1/6, of two consecutive 3s is 1/36 and so on; the probability of obtaining a series of 50 3s is very low $-1/(8.08 \times 10^{38})$. Therefore, many scientists believe that the universe has been fine tuned for life to exist. We will look for those evidences of fine tuning right from the big bang to the formation of the earth, and from emergence of life on the earth to the evolution of human beings.

A Journey from the Big Bang to the Formation of Galaxies

At the big bang, the universe was infinitely hot and dense but it cooled rapidly. We know from Einstein that energy and matter are equivalent and one can be converted into another. At such high temperature, the photons were continuously colliding with one another producing pairs of particles and anti-particles. Particles in turn got annihilated by coming into touch with anti-particles creating a flash of energy, that is, photons. Thus, equilibrium was preserved between the two processes. Since protons and antiprotons are heavy, the temperature at which such a pair is created is very high - of the order of 10 trillion degree centigrade. Therefore, the creation of proton-antiproton pairs ceased as soon as the temperature fell below 10 trillion degree centigrade, that is, during the first ten thousandth of a second after the big bang. Ideally, equal number of protons and antiprotons should have been produced during this period as per the law of conservation of charge. (A proton has +1 unit of charge while an antiproton has –1 unit of charge.) However, something extraordinary happened and for every billion antiprotons, a billion and one protons were created. Once the temperature of the universe fell below the critical level, the existing protons and antiprotons annihilated one another leaving the excess protons to form matter subsequently.[1*]

---

*Actually this was true for protons as well as neutrons, together called baryons. Although both neutron and antineutron have zero charge, they possess opposite magnetic moment.

Lighter elementary particles like electrons, positrons, neutrinos and anti-neutrinos, however, were still being produced due to collisions between photons. Naturally they far outnumbered a tiny excess of neutrons and protons left after annihilation with antiprotons and antineutrons.

The collision between an antineutrino and a proton produces a positron and a neutron, and that between a neutrino and a neutron produces a proton and an electron. Therefore, neutrons were continuously changing into protons and vice versa, which ensured that they were equal in numbers. Protons are a bit lighter than neutrons, and therefore their conversion to neutrons require more energy. Thus it was becoming more difficult for protons to convert into neutrons as the temperature kept falling. Consequently, neutron-proton ratio began to decline with the passage of time.[2]

Nearly three minutes after the big bang, when the temperature had dropped to a billion degrees centigrade, sufficient energy was not available for the conversion from neutrons to protons. The reverse conversion had ceased prior to that. The proportion of neutrons dropped to 14% and that of protons increased to 86%. Since the production of electron-positron pairs had stopped much earlier, that is, approximately 14 seconds after the big bang, all positron-electron pairs had destroyed themselves by now except a small number of electrons that was required to balance the charge of protons. Clearly, within the first three minutes of the big bang, all antimatter had vanished from the universe.[2]

How a tiny excess of protons and neutrons, one in a billion part, was created in initial 0.0001 second of the life of universe is poorly understood, if not a mystery altogether. It is possible that antimatter, by some extraordinary chance, got lumped together in a separate enclave in the universe. Since matter and antimatter both are governed by the same physical laws, somewhere in the universe, things should be made of antimatter, but unfortunately, there is so far no evidence of it. More surprisingly, the excess of electrons over positrons was exactly the same as the excess of protons over antiprotons in order to balance the charge. Therefore, the process that produced excess protons also created more electrons than positrons.

While a free proton is stable, a free neutron decays to a proton with a half-life of 10 minutes, which means that out of a hundred neutrons, fifty will turn into protons within 10 minutes. Free neutrons continued to turn into protons even after three minutes from the big bang through this process of radioactive decay. The proportion of neutrons decreased to 13% and somewhere between the third and the fourth minute neutrons began to combine with protons to form stable nuclei of helium.[3] Clearly, the building blocks of matter were ready within four minutes of the birth of the universe, which was now a thick soup of protons, helium nuclei, electrons and photons. However, the temperature was too high for a proton to capture an electron to form a hydrogen atom or a helium nucleus to capture two electrons to form a helium atom. After a long wait of 3,80,000 years, when the expansion had brought the temperature down to approximately 2,700 degree centigrade and free negatively charged electrons did not have enough energy to resist the attractive force of positively charged nuclei, the atoms of hydrogen and helium were formed.

The excess of matter over antimatter by a tiny one part in one billion was crucial for the evolution of the universe the way it is today. If matter-antimatter symmetry was not broken in the very early universe, it would exist only in the form of energy. There would be no galaxies, no stars and no planets. If, on the other hand, the particles outnumbered antiparticles by a little more, the gravitational force would have been strong enough to cause its collapse much before galaxies, stars and planets could form. This fine tuning is almost a miracle – "if the rate of expansion [of the universe] one second after the big bang had been smaller by even one part in a hundred thousand million million, the universe would have re-collapsed before it ever reached its present size."[4] It is like our nearest star Proxima Centauri being closer to us by half a metre. It is amazing that a tiny excess of matter created during the first ten thousandth of a second has produced a giant universe, billions of light years across containing trillions of stars and planets.

Today matter is concentrated in a few pockets in the universe with vast empty space surrounding them. If all the matter in the universe could be shoved into a corner, it would occupy a very tiny, almost negligible, fraction of the universe. But we know from the earliest history of the universe, which is written in the cosmic microwave background radiation (CMB), that this was not always the case. Nearly 3,80,000 years after the big bang, when all the free electrons were captured by hydrogen and helium nuclei, photons could move freely in the universe. Earlier their movements were continuously obstructed by the free electrons and they could not travel from one place to another. The first photons overcoming the barrier of electrons, when the universe was only 3,80,000 years old, constitute the CMB that was accidentally discovered by two American scientists, Penzias and Wilson in 1964. We cannot go earlier into the history of the universe than this because no photons from earlier era can be detected.

Any hot object emits radiation and the higher the temperature of the object, higher is the frequency of radiation or conversely, smaller is the wavelength. The temperature of the universe was 3,000 K (2,727°C) – almost half the temperature at the surface of the sun – when photon decoupling took place. These photons have since taken more than 13 billion years to reach the earth as the universe is expanding. Please recall that larger the distance between two galaxies, higher is the speed with which they are moving away from each other as per Hubble's law. The wavelength of the photons has also been stretched due to the expansion of the universe by approximately a thousand times and therefore the temperature of the universe has correspondingly reduced to approximately 3 K (–270°C).

Penzias and Wilson accidentally discovered CMB when they were trying to find radio signals from Milky Way galaxy with a supersensitive, 6 metre horn-shaped antenna at Bell Labs in New Jersey. They detected a constant radio hum in the microwave range which they first thought to be some kind of interference. They eliminated all possible sources including pigeon droppings on the antenna but the background hum did not disappear. More surprisingly, it was coming uniformly from all directions in the sky. Another group of scientists at Princeton, namely, Robert H Dicke, Jim Peebles, and David Wilkinson had earlier argued that the universe should be filled with radiation in microwave range as the relic of the big bang and they were looking for precisely what Penzias and Wilson accidentally discovered. The collaboration between the two groups provided the first experimental confirmation of the big bang. The experiment found the temperature of CMB at uniform 3.5 K.[5]

The initial CMB measurement was quite rudimentary but its potential in exploring the origin of the universe was well recognised. Therefore, NASA launched Cosmic Background Explorer (COBE) satellite in 1989 to study CMB with more accuracy, which was followed by Wilkinson Microwave Anisotropy Probe (WMAP) in 2001. European Space Agency (ESA) launched Planck space observatory in 2009, which mapped CMB with even more precision. These studies revised the temperature of CMB to 2.725 K from Penzias's initial estimation of 3.5 K. More importantly, it was found that the radiation was not uniform in every direction and it did exhibit very minute fluctuations of the order of 1 part in 1,00,000. Minute variations in temperature indicate that there was a very tiny variation in the distribution of matter in the early universe.[6]

We have seen in Chapter 1 that photons, though massless, are attracted by gravity in the same manner as it acts upon matter. Photons lose energy in a gravitational field, and hence its wavelength increases. The greater the gravitational force the greater is the increase in the wavelength. (In a black hole, the gravitational force is so strong that photons lose all their energy in trying to escape from it and their wavelength becomes infinite, and thus time stands still.) Therefore, wherever matter was denser in the early universe, the photons felt greater force of attraction and lost more energy in comparison, consequently they are now detected at a slightly lower temperature in CMB.

The tiny irregularities in the distribution of matter got magnified as the universe expanded. Recall the analogy of an expanding balloon - a tiny scribble may not even be visible when the balloon is very small but as it is blown up, the scribble becomes more prominent. They were further reinforced by the action of gravity because denser regions in the universe attracted more matter from the surrounding space. The ordinary matter, at this time, was largely in the form of hydrogen and helium gas, which began to clump together in huge clouds. If the internal gas pressure of a cloud is equal to the gravitational pressure, the cloud is stable, but the cloud disperses if internal gas pressure exceeds gravitational pressure, and conversely, if gravity is stronger, it starts collapsing. Under certain conditions, a huge cloud can undergo runaway collapse if the mass of the cloud is higher than a critical level called Jeans mass. (British physicist James Jeans first proposed this theory, hence the name Jeans mass.)

In a runaway collapse, the size of the cloud shrinks due to gravitational attraction, making it denser, which further increases the gravitational pressure. Molecules begin to break down into atoms due to extreme pressure and temperature, and ultimately atoms are stripped of their electrons. Positively charged nuclei repel one another but gravitational force becomes so strong that it surpasses Coulomb's barrier and nuclei fuse together. Nuclear fusion produces enormous amount of energy that counterbalances the gravitational force, halting the runaway collapse. All stars get their energy from this process in which lighter elements turn into heavier elements, for example, hydrogen converts into helium, helium into lithium, so on and so forth. (600 million tonnes of hydrogen is burnt every second to power our sun.) The process stops when the fusion chain produces iron because it is the most stable element.

In a giant molecular cloud, runaway collapse can take place in several local regions if they satisfy Jeans conditions, thus giving birth to a collection of several stars, called a globular cluster. A galaxy contains many globular clusters – the Milky Way galaxy has roughly 150 known globular clusters, each containing millions of stars. The first stars and galaxies were formed in this manner from the gravitational collapse of giant hydrogen and helium clouds, approximately 200 million years after the big bang. When the universe was 3,80,000 years old, some portion of the CMB radiation was in the visible range. If a human being was present in that era, he would see uniform glow of red light coming from all directions. This diminished as CMB shifted to the infrared part of the spectrum due to the expansion of the universe. Gradually, the universe became a completely dark place as infrared radiation is not visible to human eyes, and it remained so until the emergence of the first stars.[7]

Thus a tiny variation of 1 part in 1,00,000 in the distribution of matter is responsible for the formation of all large scale structures in the universe. "If our universe had started off completely smooth and uniform, it would have remained so throughout its expansion. After ten billion years, it would contain thinly spread dark matter, and hydrogen and helium gas so rarefied that there was less than one atom in each cubic metre. It would be cold and dull: no galaxies, therefore no stars, no periodic table, no complexity, certainly no people."[8] Conversely, if the density fluctuations in the early universe were more pronounced, the matter would clump together more easily and rapidly into clouds of enormous size:

> They wouldn't fragment into stars but would instead collapse into vast black holes, each much heavier than an entire cluster of galaxies in our universe. Any surviving gas would get so hot that it would emit intense X-rays and gamma rays. Galaxies (even if they managed to form) would be much more tightly bound than the actual galaxies in our universe. Stars would be packed too close together and buffeted too frequently to retain stable planetary systems. (For similar reasons, solar systems are not able to exist very close to the centre of our own galaxy, where the stars are in a close-packed swarm compared with our less-central locality).[9]

Much like a living being, a star is born; it grows and finally ends up in a highly dense object or explodes in a supernova. Typically a star of the size of the sun collapses in a white dwarf of the size of the earth. A low mass star generates energy from nuclear fusion of hydrogen into helium. When hydrogen is exhausted, the star begins to collapse; and it becomes smaller and smaller until the gravitational attraction is balanced by the repulsive force between electrons. A star the size of the sun can fuse helium to form carbon, and still larger stars can produce heavier elements up to iron though the process of nuclear fusion. But once all the fuel is exhausted, it begins to collapse very rapidly leading to massive explosion called supernova. Heavier elements like carbon, oxygen and iron are thrown into space, which becomes raw material for the birth of a new star. It is our good fortune that the sun is not among the first stars that were born; rather it was created more than 10 billion years after the big bang, from the ashes of earlier stars, and therefore our solar system contains elements like carbon, oxygen, iron etc vital for the creation of life.

Milky Way Galaxy and Our Solar System

The formation of the Milky Way galaxy began 9 billion years ago. It is a spiral galaxy 1,00,000 light years across with several spiral arms and the sun is located approximately 27,000 light years away from the centre of the galaxy. The galaxy rotates on its centre roughly once every 225 million years. The sun's distance from the galactic centre is of great significance for the existence of life. The closer one gets to the centre, more dangerous it becomes for life to exist because of violent cosmic activities like explosion of dying stars, bombardment of comets and intense bursts of harmful radiation. Farther we go from centre, the chance of stars having heavy elements essential to support life gets dimmer. Therefore, a very small portion of a galaxy is capable of sustaining life or complex life, which is known as the galactic habitable zone. It has been estimated that this zone for the Milky Way galaxy extends from 22,830 light years to 29,350 light years from the centre.[10]

The solar system was formed much later – it is only 4.5 billion years old. A vast cloud of gas and dust – the remnants of an earlier generation of stars – started to collapse and took the shape of a huge disk. As it collapsed it spun faster and faster until nuclear fusion was ignited in the central region, which formed the sun. The periphery of the disk split into rings and accreted matter from the surrounding to create earth and other planets, moons and asteroids. Within a billion years of the formation of the earth, the conditions became hospitable for the emergence of life on it. However, that happened only because many things fortuitously turned out to be just right on our planet.

Miraculously, the Earth has Everything to Support Life

Water is essential for life because a variety of substances easily dissolve in liquid water, making it an excellent carrier of nutrients from one part to another part of organisms. It also helps in removing waste material from the body. Therefore, a habitable planet must have the temperature within 0°C-100°C for the emergence of life. (A rare species of archaea, Pyrolobus fumarii, was discovered in 1997 inside a hydrothermal vent in Atlantic Ocean, 3,650 metre below the surface at 113°C. Another strain of the species has been found even at 122°C, but no form of life is known to exist beyond this temperature; similarly, no species have been found to live at a temperature below -15°C.) Fortunately, the earth maintains a comfortable average temperature of 16°C. It also revolves around the sun in a nearly circular orbit, which ensures that the temperature does not vary greatly during its yearly revolution. Venus, our neighbour closer to the sun, has an average temperature of 467°C whereas Mars, away from the sun, an average temperature of -50°C. Not surprisingly, no sign of life has so far been detected from our two closest neighbours.

The atmosphere also plays a very key role in maintaining a comfortable temperature on the earth by trapping heat. The moon is also at the same distance from the sun as the earth is but it has no atmosphere, and therefore day temperature goes as high as 122°C and night temperature plummets to -173°C. The release of greenhouse gases from human activities like burning of fossil fuels is causing global warming, which now poses a danger to human civilization. The concentration of carbon dioxide in the atmosphere has risen from pre-industrial level of 0.028% to 0.04% by volume, which is largely responsible for the rise in average temperature at the earth's surface by 1°C during the period. The average temperature on the surface of the earth would almost double to 31°C if the concentration of carbon dioxide increased to 0.10%, and this calculation is based on past record when the atmosphere actually contained more carbon dioxide:

> What was Earth's climate like at the time of past elevated CO_2 [carbon dioxide]? Consider one example when CO_2 was

> ~1000 ppmv [0.10%] at ~35 million years ago. Temperature data for this time period indicate that tropical to subtropical sea surface temperatures were in the range of 35° to 40°C (versus present-day temperatures of ~30°C) and that sea surface temperatures at polar latitudes in the South Pacific were 20° to 25°C (versus modern temperatures of ~5°C) ... the global annual mean temperature at this time can be estimated to be ~31°C, versus 15°C during pre-industrial times (around 1750). Thus, Earth was ~16°C warmer at 30 to 40 Ma [million years].[11]

Mere doubling of CO_2 can be catastrophic for life on the earth, and so would be its decline. Therefore, our planet is not only at the right distance from the sun but also contains the right amount of greenhouse gases to keep its temperature in the habitable range. The atmosphere also regulates pressure: it is so thick on Venus that the pressure is 90 times more than the earth. We would be simultaneously crushed and roasted if we ever landed on the planet. As we climb up to higher altitude on the earth, the atmospheric pressure decreases. At the top of Mount Everest the pressure is almost one third of that at the sea level. We, therefore, experience difficulty in breathing at higher altitude as the lungs are not able to suck enough air from the low pressure atmosphere, reducing the supply of oxygen to the body. What will happen on the surface of the moon where the pressure is negligible because it hardly has any atmosphere? A person will die of asphyxiation within minutes, if not seconds.

The earth's atmosphere also acts as a shield that protects us from falling meteors (shooting stars) by burning them up when they pass through it. The particles in the atmosphere offer resistance to meteors and heat them up – much in the same manner as rubbing of two stones produces heat. When the temperature crosses ignition point, the meteors start burning. Very few meteors therefore survive the atmosphere and are able to hit the earth. Without the atmosphere, the earth would face a constant bombardment of meteors – it would be like walking in a hailstorm without an umbrella.

The atmosphere is also a filter that allows sunlight in the visible range (wavelength of 400-700 nanometre) to pass through but blocks both ultraviolet (UV) and infrared light from reaching the earth's surface. The UV rays are absorbed largely by the ozone layer in the atmosphere and infrared by the greenhouse gases. In the absence of the ozone layer, we would be exposed to harmful UV rays, which may cause damage to eyes and skin. The ozone layer is not a single sheet of uniform thickness that covers the earth. Ozone molecules are widely dispersed in the atmosphere from 15-30 km above the earth's surface. However if the entire ozone were to be packed in a single layer, the average thickness of the sheet would be 3 millimetre, less than a third of a centimetre. In 1985, it was discovered that the ozone layer over Antarctica had substantially thinned, which spurred the global community to sign the Montreal Protocol to phase out ozone depleting substances.

The magnetic field around the earth protects us from dangerous charged particles, mostly electrons and protons emanating from the sun, by deflecting them away. A few of them manage to reach the earth's upper atmosphere and collide with the molecules of oxygen and nitrogen, producing brilliant colours known as the northern lights:

> In addition to visible and ultraviolet light, the sun emits many other forms of radiation. High energy electrons and protons continuously stream from the sun; this stream is commonly called the solar wind. The sun emits these particles with velocities between 200 km/s and 800 km/s, depending on where you are relative to the sun's equator and the solar activity cycle. When these charged particles encounter matter, such as living tissue, they deposit their energy as they slow down and stop therein.... [The] process does significant damage to any living tissue in which it occurs. Even short-term exposure to unfiltered sunlight can cause mutations and cancer. Moderate to long-term exposure results in significant cell damage and death.[12]

The reason for the earth's magnetism is not exactly known, but it is widely attributed to some sort of dynamo effect. The outer core of the earth, which is 2,300 km thick, contains iron and nickel in molten form. The temperature of the core decreases towards the surface of the earth. As a result, the hotter liquid rises up and the cooler matter sinks down. The earth also spins on its axis, causing the liquid to swirl. Since molten iron and nickel contain many free electrons, they too move from the core towards the surface and vice versa. This movement of electrons produces electric current, which, in turn, creates the magnetic field.

The first atmosphere of the earth contained hydrogen and helium, much like the present day atmosphere of larger planets, that is, Jupiter, Saturn, Uranus and Neptune. Gravity on the earth is not strong enough, however, to retain light gases, and therefore they gradually escaped. The second atmosphere was formed by the gases spewed from numerous volcanoes that erupted due to intense tectonic activities on the earth. It closely resembled what the atmosphere of Mars and Venus is today, rich in carbon dioxide, which constitutes more than 95% of their atmosphere, and a small amount of nitrogen gas. However, our present atmosphere contains 78% nitrogen, 21% oxygen and only 0.04% carbon dioxide, and this has happened due to absorption of carbon dioxide by the oceans and its conversion to oxygen by plants.

Rains carried carbon dioxide in the atmosphere to the oceans where it gradually dissolved in the water. It reacted chemically with calcium present in the crust and turned into limestone in a slow process lasting millions of years. (Since water is not available on Venus, its atmosphere still contains a large proportion of carbon dioxide.) When blue-green bacteria (cyanobacteria) first appeared in the bosom of the oceans, the conversion of carbon dioxide to oxygen began because, as we know, plants make food (carbohydrate) from carbon dioxide in the presence of sunlight, and emit oxygen. The oxygen could not make its way to the atmosphere but initially reacted with metals and organic materials present on the earth. As plant life multiplied, the rate of photosynthesis exceeded the rate of oxidation of metals, and oxygen began to appear in the atmosphere:

> Evidence for a permanent rise to appreciable concentrations of O_2 [oxygen] in the atmosphere sometime between 2.4 and 2.1 billion years ago began to accumulate as early as the 1960s. This step increase, now popularly known as the 'Great Oxidation Event' or GOE, left clear fingerprints in the rock record. For example, the first appearance of rusty red soils on land and the disappearance of easily oxidized minerals such as pyrite (FeS_2) from ancient stream beds both point to the presence of oxygen in the atmosphere.[13]

The level of oxygen however continued to be low compared to today for a very long period of time, but was sufficient to create a layer of ozone to protect life from harmful ultraviolet radiation of the sun. Another spike in the concentration of oxygen took place ~800-600 million years ago that increased the concentration near the present level. It is evident that chemical and biological activity changed the composition of our atmosphere over a few billion years.

The story of water on earth is more complicated with little agreement among the scientists on how it arrived. The dominant hypothesis has been that it was brought by comets and asteroids. After all, earth in its formative stage was too close to solar nebulae to retain any water, as it would have evaporated due to extreme heat. Comets and asteroids carry a lot of water and the baby earth was hit by them in great numbers, which lends credence to the hypothesis, but this is now being challenged as new evidence to the contrary is emerging – the composition of water found in comets does not match with the ocean water.

An ordinary water molecule is made of two atoms of hydrogen and one atom of oxygen. However another type of water, known as heavy water, contains two atoms of deuterium – a deuterium atom has a proton and a neutron unlike a hydrogen atom which has only a proton – and one atom of oxygen. Scientists have found that the proportion of heavy water in most comets is substantially higher than the ocean water. Although water has been found for the first time on 24 Themis, an asteroid, its composition is unknown. More evidence is required before it is said with any degree of confidence that asteroids indeed delivered water to the earth. This leaves alive the possibility of water being present since the beginning of the earth, safely hidden in the planetesimals – minute planets that coalesced to form the earth.

Our planet, therefore, possessed all the elements necessary to support life – right temperature and pressure, water and the right atmosphere. Life must have begun in the bosom of the ocean, safe from harmful ultraviolet radiation of the sun. Cyanobacteria, the first species to emerge, used amply available carbon dioxide for food, and as they multiplied, the conversion from carbon dioxide to oxygen accelerated. Gradually, oxygen began to accumulate in the atmosphere, a thin layer of ozone was formed and animal life appeared on the earth. The proposition that the conditions were favourable on the earth to support life is straightforward and easily testable – alter those conditions and life ceases to exist. But this is not the same as saying that such conditions would necessarily lead to creation of life. If such conditions existed elsewhere in the universe, would life always sprout from non-living molecules and evolve to more and more complex species as happened on the earth? These are tough questions to answer, primarily because how exactly life arose on the earth is not known.

Mystery of Emergence of Life on the Earth

In Chapter 2, we discussed in some detail the basic constituents of life – DNA, RNA and protein, and what might have come first. RNA first hypothesis is attractive because RNA performs both functions: it contains genetic information and catalyses biological reactions. RNA is a complex macromolecule, a long chain of four different types of nucleotides, namely adenine, guanine, cytosine and uracil. However, even if the hypothesis is correct, there is no clue as to how RNA macromolecule was created in the first place. The odd, that a self-replicating RNA macromolecule was randomly created from a prebiotic soup of nucleotides is very low, and even if such a miraculous thing happened, there was no guarantee that few chance molecules would weave an entire RNA world:

> Some unconditional supporters of the original version of the RNA world take refuge in the notion of a 'flick of chance'. They imagine a few RNA molecules arising somewhere by an almost miraculous combination of circumstances. Such an event would, in their eyes, have been enough for the whole process to be launched, thanks to the ability of RNA to self-replicate and display catalysis. Such a view does not hold water. First, the very hypothesis of RNA arising by some chance event is chemically implausible. Moreover, having a little RNA obviously does not suffice for making more. The term 'self-replication' is misleading in this respect, as it confounds two entities: information and synthesis. RNA provides only the former.[14]

There are two incontrovertible facts: one, that the earliest sign of life from fossil records dates back to more than 3.5 billion years ago[15] and the building blocks of life contain elements like carbon, hydrogen, oxygen, nitrogen and phosphorus, and two, that these elements were present on the earth in some compound forms like methane, ammonia, carbon dioxide and phosphate etc. But the story between these two dots is absolutely hazy – there are many hypotheses but no path to connect the two dots. How lifeless molecules acquired the ability to replicate and grow is a question that still haunts science. However, all that can be said is that the creation of life from inanimate matter is not a common event on the earth, and therefore, the conclusion that the circumstances must have been finely-tuned, whatever was the mechanism, is inescapable.

First Evolutionary Leap

After that – between the origin of life and the emergence of Homo sapiens (modern man) – there are some critical evolutionary leaps that too remain poorly understood, though the things are not as obscure, and the contours of evolution are broadly known. Unicellular organisms, bacteria and archaea, ruled the earth and life remained struck in this simplest form for approximately two billion years. Then suddenly a new type of cell was born, having separate compartments called organelles (small organs) within the cell to perform specialised functions. This type of cell is called eukaryote, which literally means 'true kernel'. In eukaryotes, the nucleus contains genetic information and mitochondria produces energy in contrast to prokaryotes which do not have nucleus, mitochondria and other organelles. Eukaryotes are typically a thousand times larger than the prokaryotes and capable of sexual reproduction. Moreover, eukaryotic chromosomes contain a lot more junk DNA, the DNA that does not code for protein. They are, therefore, a great deal more complex than prokaryotes.

"How this complexity evolved is a major enigma of evolutionary biology, which is, of course, all the more tantalizing, thanks to the inescapable parochial interest. After all, when we explore the origin of eukaryotes, we are looking into our own origins."[16] The endosymbiotic hypothesis, which is currently the most accepted one, believes that eukaryotic cells evolved from the uniting of two prokaryotic cells. An archaea might have attacked and engulfed a bacterium but it proved to be mutually beneficial to each other, and the engulfed bacteria gradually developed into a specialized internal organ called mitochondria within the host cell. The transition from prokaryotes to eukaryotes in the evolution process is of great significance because it paved the way for the emergence of multicellular organisms on the earth.

Nick Lane, a British biochemist, a staunch proponent of endosymbiosis, argues brilliantly that the standard process of evolution did not produce the eukaryotes because if they "had evolved most of their complexity in the course of adapting to distinct ways of life in divergent populations, then this long history should be reflected in their distinctive internal structures too. But look inside ... and you will see that all eukaryotes are made of basically the same components."[17] The prokaryotes have existed on the earth for more than 3.5 billion years and "yet in all this immense duration, neither the bacteria nor the archaea became anything else: they remained stubbornly simple in their structure and way of life."[18] Clearly, the emergence of a complex cell was a freak accident in our history without which life would have been eternally consigned to the simplicity of a bacteria.

Species Go Multicellular

It took another billion years for the next evolutionary leap to occur – from unicellularity to multicellularity. A multicellular organism is vastly more complex than a single-celled organism because the cells have to stick together in a three dimensional structure, develop a mechanism to communicate with one another and share food. Different types of cells perform specialised functions like movement, reproduction, conversion from food to energy etc. The blueprint of development – when and where different types of cells grow and eventually die – is written in the DNA of a multicellular organism. In contrast, a unicellular organism multiplies endlessly by simple cell division producing exact replicas of the parent cell, and in that sense a unicellular organism never dies.

"Multicellularity has evolved independently in ten different major clades and over 25 times in individual lineages within these clades, each of which had unicellular ancestral condition."[19] The actual number of times multicellular organisms evolved from unicellular ancestors could be even more as some fossil records may not have survived or lie hidden in the bosom of the earth. A recent study has shown that a single genetic mutation may have caused the evolution of multicellular organisms.[20] However, only three lineages succeeded in spawning wide varieties of complex organisms – animals, plants and fungi. Why only three attempts succeeded in the long history of over 3.5 billion years is yet unclear. Why existing single-celled organisms are not evolving into multicellular organisms? Has mutation of genes stopped playing the trick because all possible combinations of mutations in single-celled organisms have been exhausted over time? If so, it leads to an interesting conclusion: that theoretically unicellular life would evolve over a long period of time to a few multicellular organisms; others would revert to unicellularism or become extinct.

Cambrian Explosion

This brings us to the last of the big leaps forward: the Cambrian explosion. But before we do that a little understanding of grouping organisms on the basis of shared characteristics will be helpful in appreciating its real significance. The highest level of grouping of organisms is domain – there are only three domains of life: bacteria, archaea and eukarya. The lowest level is species – a group that can breed among themselves to produce offspring. And in between there are kingdom, phylum, class, order, family and genus. Phylum is a grouping based on the type of body plan, for example, humans and other vertebrates are classified under Chordata phylum as we have a nerve cord that runs down the back.

The Cambrian explosion refers to the sudden appearance of a large number of animal species in the fossil records of

Cambrian period that started 550 million years and ended 490 million years ago. This unique event is greatly responsible for the variety of life around us:

> Our planet was without animal life for the first 3.5 billion years of its existence and was without animals large enough to leave a visible fossil record for nearly 4 billion years. But when, 550 million years ago, sizable and diverse animal life finally burst into the oceans, it did so with a figurative bang – in a relatively sudden event known as the Cambrian Explosion. Over a relatively short interval of time, all of the animal phyla (the categories of animal life characterized by unique body plans, such as arthropods, mollusks, and chordates) either evolved or first appear in the fossil record.... The rate of evolutionary innovation and new species formation during the Cambrian Explosion has never been equalled. The prior animal diversification must have involved very few species, each growing to a very small size; the Cambrian Explosion, on the other hand, produced huge numbers of new species, many with completely novel body plans.[21]

More interestingly the Cambrian period marked the end of innovation in 'body types' since no new phyla has emerged thereafter. The Cambrian period ended with mass extinction of species and yet when new species emerged later, the body types remained unchanged. The diversification took place at the level of species but not phyla. Either mutation ceased to create new phyla or the environment did not select them. The forces of evolution continued to work incessantly in creating more complex species, punctuated by several temporary setbacks – at least in five of them half of the species were destroyed.[22] (The dinosaurs were completely wiped out 65 million years ago most probably due to collision with an asteroid.) Fish evolved nearly 500 million years ago, followed by amphibians, reptiles and finally mammals. The great ape family consisting of humans, chimpanzees, gorillas, and orangutans appeared only 15 million years ago and Homo erectus, first species to walk upright, 2 million years ago. In 3.5-4 billion years of the history of life on the earth, our (Homo sapiens) presence has been for an insignificant period, only 2,00,000 years.

Many possible explanations have been offered for the Cambrian explosion. Some argue that the level of oxygen in earth's atmosphere rose to the modern value ~800-600 million years ago, that is, just before the Cambrian explosion. Oxygen allowed the evolution of larger organisms because it was able to cater to their higher requirement of energy. They were able to form hard skeletons for the first time. Others contend that the change in composition of sea water triggered it by providing hitherto unavailable nutrients. Still others believe that some critical evolutionary limit was breached which accelerated the process. The precise reason for the Cambrian explosion is hard to determine; possibly, it was the result of a complex interplay of several factors.

Fundamental Constants are Finely Tuned

Be it tiny excess of matter over antimatter, a small irregularity in the distribution of matter in the early universe, the location of the sun in the Milky Way galaxy, the distance of the earth from the sun, the right composition of the earth's atmosphere and many more, it looks as if everything conspired to make human life possible on the earth. If a little error happened at any place in this long journey I would not be writing these words. Imagine the hailstorm of asteroids and comets that living beings cheated; imagine the burst of gamma rays that they survived; and imagine the mass extinctions that the species suffered. Think of a chance meeting between an archaea and a bacterium that created eukaryotes.

This much, therefore, is certain that we have arrived treading on a razor's edge.

Physical phenomena are governed by well-defined laws, which are expressed in mathematical equations. The evidence of tuning, therefore, can be found in the equations, which contain constants having specific values. Why are those values what they are? Why should gravitational constant G in Newton's law of universal gravitation have a value of 6.674×10^{-11}? What would happen if the value G were a bit more or less? The argument can be extended to any other fundamental constant. Martin Rees, a British cosmologist, has argued that the essence of fine tuning can be elegantly captured in just six numbers: the ratio of electromagnetic force to gravitational force, a number that defines how firmly atomic nuclei bind together, the ratio of density of matter in the universe to critical density required to halt its expansion, the cosmological constant in Einstein's general theory of relativity, the ratio of total energy required to break stars, galaxies, and clusters of galaxies held together by gravity to their total rest mass energy ($E = mc^2$), and finally the number of spatial dimensions in the universe. These numbers are fundamental in the sense that they are unrelated to one another:

> These six numbers constitute a 'recipe' for a universe. Moreover, the outcome is sensitive to their values: if any one of them were to be 'untuned', there would be no stars and no life.... Perhaps there are some connections between these numbers. At the moment, however, we cannot predict any one of them from the values of the others. Nor do we know whether some 'theory of everything' will eventually yield a formula that interrelates them, or that specifies them uniquely. I have highlighted these six because each plays a crucial and distinctive role in our universe, and together they determine how the universe evolves and what its internal potentialities are....[23]

The apparent fine tuning of the universe has long puzzled scientists, and since there is no credible explanation, it has led to the formulation of the anthropic principle. The principle has two popular versions. The weak version of anthropic principle simply states that the universe is the way it is because if it were not, we would not be here to observe it. However, it is one thing to argue that our existence in this universe is a sheer coincidence, quite another to conclude that it has been purposely designed to bring us into existence. The strong anthropic principle argues that we are the cause of the universe. In the former, we are at the periphery, and in the latter at the centre, being the compelling reason for the universe to come into existence. And this raises the question: are we alone in the universe?

Are We Alone in the Universe?

There are, even according to conservative estimates, at least 100 billion galaxies in the universe and our galaxy alone contains 100-400 billion stars. Since nearly all stars have planets, their number will be of the order of 10^{22}, that is, 1 followed by 22 zeroes, a mind boggling number. Of this, scientists estimate that billions of planets are earth-like. Could some of them host carbon based life? Those who believe that life is a necessary consequence of chemistry argue that given similar conditions, it will invariably arise. Others argue exactly the opposite: the probability of creation of life is so low that even billions of earth-like planets are not enough for it to emerge anywhere else in the universe. This dilemma can only be resolved if we actually find life somewhere else in the universe, which today seems impossible. Even if billions of planets in the universe are teeming with life, there is no direct way of finding them because of huge distances between stars and galaxies. Our fastest space vehicle hasn't breached the speed limit of 100 km per second and at current speeds it will take more than 15,000 years to travel to the nearest star.

What about an intelligent species from another planet sending a radio signal which can be detected on the earth? Humans have developed such technology fairly recently. Had the earth been inundated with radio signals coming from extra-terrestrial life 500 years back, we would have certainly missed them. If an intelligent species from Andromeda galaxy sends a signal today towards the earth, it will reach us 25,40,000 years later, when humans may not be around to receive them. For such a thing to happen, the two species should not only exist in two different epochs but the period between them should also be equal to the time taken by radio signals to travel from one place to another. This indeed will be an event of extremely low probability. Further, we have no idea whether any other type of life, which is not based on carbon and is completely different from life on the earth, is possible. Therefore, the question whether we are alone in universe or not may continue to remain within the realm of speculation.

If life exists or has ever existed elsewhere in the universe, the strong anthropic principle becomes indefensible, but the weak version still holds. However, if the earth indeed is alone in the universe with no life anywhere else, the strong principle is a tempting offer to restore the centrality of the earth in the cosmos, which was dislodged from its position by Copernicus. But if that be the case, the immensity of earth's loneliness would be hard to fathom. The universe is spread across a length of the order of 10^{24} km whereas the diameter of the earth is 12,742 km only and the earth is one of 10^{22} planets in the entire universe. Its loneliness in the vast cosmos would really be scary. It is like you are the only person on the earth with all the oceans, mountains and deserts to yourself. Haven't we all dreaded being marooned on an island, or lost in a desert! How would it feel to live all alone on the earth!

Future of Mankind

Will humanity survive forever or the run of good luck come to an end? There are several dangers lurking on the way. We may be wiped out in a nuclear holocaust; climate change can be potentially disastrous; we can run out of resources; super volcanoes, massive earthquakes or tsunamis can erase our existence from the face of the earth. Dinosaurs became extinct 65 million years ago when a giant asteroid collided with earth and such an event in the future cannot be ruled out. The longer humanity survives, the greater is the probability of such an asteroid hitting the earth, but NASA tracks asteroids likely to pass near the earth and the potentially dangerous ones can be diverted. The liquid core of the earth can solidify and the earth can lose its magnetism rendering us vulnerable to radiation. Gamma rays burst from a nearby supernova explosion can strip the earth of its magnetism and destroy living beings on it. And if we survive all this, the sun is getting hotter – the sun was only 70% luminous when it was young. In a billion years from now the temperature on the earth would increase so much that oceans would evaporate. The sun would begin to swell and ultimately, in about seven billion years, its size would increase so much that the earth would be engulfed. It would shine 3,000 times brighter. The earth would return to the womb of sun from where it was born.

One may argue, at least theoretically, that human beings can develop technology to nudge the earth in a different orbit farther from the sun or emigrate to Mars, but that will not help much either because the sun, after attaining its maximum size and luminosity, will soon run out of fuel. In the absence of a counterforce to balance gravity, it will begin to collapse and turn into a white dwarf, the size of the earth. The solar system will become a cold and dark place without a source of energy. All life will cease to exist. To survive, we will need to escape to a planet outside the solar system.

The ultimate fate of the universe is not yet known but it depends on the proportion of ordinary matter, dark matter and dark energy in the universe. If the universe contains more than enough matter, it will stop expanding at some stage, begin to contract and end up in a big crunch – the opposite of the big bang. If the proportion of matter is just enough, the expansion will progressively slow down but never become zero. The galaxies will get farther apart and average temperature will reach closer and closer to zero. All stars will gradually die. The universe will become dark again. Finally, if dark energy dominates the universe, its expansion will accelerate and galaxies will fly away from one another at exponentially increasing speed. The expansion of space-time will create more dark energy, which will further increase the acceleration. Eventually, dark energy will become so much that it will rip galaxies apart and stars will explode. Ultimately, dark energy will overpower electromagnetic force and break molecules and atoms too. Matter as we know will cease to exist.

I would argue that the 'fine tuning' is not only a feature at the cosmic scale but is also equally relevant in day to day life. The evidence of balance is everywhere, in economy, in polity, in society, and in life generally. When we go to a hospital for a routine health check-up, we know that all parameters must remain within a narrow range, and any value outside the permissible range is a sign of some malaise. In economy, the trade-off between growth and inflation is the principal concern of central banks all over the world. In order to boost growth, central banks resort to easy money supply, but this fuels inflation. While the benefit of growth is not shared equally by all people, inflation affects everyone, particularly the poor. Similarly, a fine balance has to be struck between equity and efficiency. Too strong reliance on equity hurts efficiency but solely focusing on efficiency creates inequality in society. In a democratic polity, there are usually two or three major parties differing in ideological persuasion. If one veers towards the Left, other veers towards the Right, and a see-saw battle between them continues.

Striking a Fine Balance in Life

There is an old saying in Sanskrit: *Ati sarvatra varjayet*. Excess of everything is bad. Sita was abducted because she was too beautiful and Ravana was killed because of excess pride.

Even excess truth can be harmful. If somebody is being chased by a killer, and he takes refuge in your house, you will not let it be known to the killer. Therefore, one should refrain from indulging in excess. The same thought is echoed by Lao Tzu. In Osho's words:

> If you are in love and twenty-four hours a day you are after your lover, and you move to the extreme as lovers do, everything will be destroyed. You will destroy love yourself, because it is too much. It becomes unbearable…. Food nourishes, but eat too much and food becomes poison, it kills. That which was a [sic] nourishment becomes a poison and a killer…. If you are laughing twenty-four hours a day, your laughter will become neurotic. It will no longer be a laughter – you will go mad.[24]

One way to look at 'fine-tunings' in the universe is that they are a series of independent events, but the trouble with this view is that the probability of occurrence of this is very low indeed. The other way is to think that these 'fine tunings' are not a succession of events but were programmed in the force that created the universe in the first place. We have seen in the previous chapter that scientists are trying to unite the four fundamental forces into one force, called the Theory of Everything (ToE). They believe that at the very instant of the big bang the temperature was so high that there was only one fundamental force. As the universe cooled, the gravitational force was the first one to get decoupled, followed by strong nuclear force. Finally electroweak force also split into two, namely, weak nuclear force and electromagnetic force. If the ToE is described by a set of mathematical equations, could they contain the ultimate code for the evolution of the universe, much in the same way DNA in a single zygote cell contains the blueprint of the development of a person. This view is strengthened by Hindu-Buddhist philosophy, which conceives the universe as one, undifferentiated whole, and in which the various components are in perfect harmony and balance with one another. Hindu philosophy views the universe as a giant net woven by Indra:

> The metaphor of Indra's Net originates from the *Atharva Veda* (one of four *Vedas*), which likens the world to a net woven by great [*Vedic*] deity Shakra or Indra. The net is said to be infinite, and to spread in all directions with no beginning or end. At each node of the net is a jewel, so arranged that every jewel reflects all the other jewels. No jewel exists by itself independently of the rest. Everything is related to everything else; nothing is isolated.... Every jewel in Indra's Net is a microcosm of the whole net; every component is the cause of the whole and also the effect of the whole....[25]

There is a wonderful concept in Buddhism: *Pratitya samutpada* or dependent origination, which does not believe that cause and effect are separate. The cause is also an effect and the effect is also a cause and both are dependent on each other. Everything arises together. "This is, because that is. This is not, because that is not. This comes to be, because that comes to be. This ceases to be, because that ceases to be."[26] Zen Master, Thich Nhat Hanh illustrates beautifully:

> For a table to exist, we need wood, a carpenter, time, skilfulness, and many other causes. And each of these causes needs other causes to be. The wood needs the forest, the sunshine, the rain, and so on. The carpenter needs his parents, breakfast, fresh air, and so on. And each of those things, in turn, has to be brought about by other conditions. If we continue to look in this way, we'll see that nothing has been left out. Everything in the cosmos has come together to bring us this table. Looking deeply at the sunshine, the leaves of the tree, and the clouds, we can see the table. The one can be seen in the all, and the all can be seen in the one.[27]

The universe has emerged from *shunyata* or nothingness, therefore, it contains within itself multiple opposing tendencies, all kept in a fine balance by *rta*, the cosmic order. One jewel in Indra's Net cannot be disturbed without perturbing the others. A small deviation here creates ripples there until *rta* is restored, and in this elegantly woven net lies its beauty that we marvel at.

Notes and References

1. *The First Three Minutes: A Modern View of the Origin of the Universe* by Steven Weinberg, pp 95-6, Basic Books, New York, 1993.
2. *Ibid*, pp 101-12.
3. *Ibid*, p 110.
4. *The Illustrated A Brief History of Time* by Stephen Hawking, p 156, Bantam Books, New York, 1996.
5. *The First Three Minutes: A Modern View of the Origin of the Universe* by Steven Weinberg, pp 45-9, Basic Books, New York, 1993.
6. *Surveying the Skies: How Astronomers Map the Universe* by Gareth Wynn-Williams, p 90, Springer International Publishing, Switzerland, 2016.
7. *Exploring the Invisible Universe: From Black Holes to Superstrings* by Belal E Baaaquie and Frederick H Willeboordse, p 159, World Scientific, Singapore, 2015.
8. *Just Six Numbers: The Deep Forces that Shape the Universe* by Martin Rees, p 117, Basic Books, New York, 2000.
9. *Ibid*, p 115.
10. "The Galactic Habitable Zone of the Milky Way and M31 from Chemical Evolution Models with Gas Radial Flows", E Spitoni, F Matteucci, A Sozzetti, *Monthly Notices of the Royal Astronomical Society*, Vol 440, No 3, 2014, pp 2588-98.
11. "Lessons from Earth's Past", Jeffrey Kiehl, *Science*, Vol 331, No 6014, 2011, pp 158-9.
12. *Paradise Regained: The Regreening of Earth* by Gregory Matloff, C Bangs and Les Johnson, p 4, Copernicus Books, New York, 2010.
13. "The Rise of Oxygen in Earth's Early Ocean and Atmosphere", Timothy W Lyons, Christopher T Reinhard and Noah J Planavsky, *Nature*, Vol 506, No 7488, 2014, p 307.
14. *Life Evolving: Molecules, Mind, and Meaning* by Christian de Duve, p 61, Oxford University Press, New York, 2002.
15. *The Vital Question: Why is Life the Way It Is* by Nick Lane, p 29, Profile Books, London, 2016.

16. *The Logic of Chance: The Nature and Origin of Biological Evolution* by Eugene V Koonin, p 171, Pearson Education, Inc, USA, 2011.

17. *The Vital Question: Why is Life the Way It Is* by Nick Lane, p 34, Profile Books, London, 2016.

18. *Ibid,* p 50.

19. *Multicellularity: Origins and Evolution,* edited by Karl J Niklas and Stuart A Newman, Preface, xxi, the MIT Press, Cambridge, 2016.

20. "Evolution of an Ancient Protein Function involved in Organized Multicellularity in Animals", Douglas P Anderson, et al. eLife 2016;5:e10147

21. *Rare Earth: Why Complex Life is Uncommon in the Universe* by Peter D Ward and Donald Brownlee, pp 125-6, Copernicus Books, New York, 2003.

22. *Ibid,* pp 142, 152 and 161.

23. *Just Six Numbers: The Deep Forces That Shape the Universe* by Martin Rees, pp 3-4, Basic Books, New York, 2000.

24. *Absolute Tao: Subtle is the Way to Love, Happiness and Truth* by Osho, pp 99-100, Osho International, Mumbai, 2012.

25. *Indra's Net: Defending Hinduism's Philosophical Unity* by Rajiv Malhotra, pp 4-5, HarperCollins Publishers India, 2016.

26. *The Heart of the Buddha's Teaching: Transforming Suffering into Peace, Joy, and Liberation* by Thich Nhat Hanh, p 221, Harmony Books, New York, 2015.

27. *Ibid,* p 222.

7

Conclusion

At macroscopic (very large) level quantum mechanics is irrelevant and at microscopic (very small) level gravity is insignificant. Just calculate the gravitational force between the nucleus and the electron of a hydrogen atom; it is 10^{39} times less than the electromagnetic forces between them. Therefore, gravity and quantum mechanics can exist separately in different domains without any apparent contradiction. But the universe was incredibly small just after the big bang and its entire mass was packed into an infinitesimal space. It is not possible to ignore the effect of gravitational force between particles in such a situation. Therefore, scientists have to reconcile quantum theory with gravity because the two are entirely different from each other. While quantum theory is probabilistic, gravity is entirely deterministic. In quantum theory, energy distribution is discrete unlike gravity. (Recall that Einstein's photoelectric effect has demonstrated that energy is emitted only in packets.) Let us assume that a source is emitting only red light. The energy carried by each photon would be 2.8×10^{-19} joule (Let us define it as one unit). Clearly, a source of red light can emit energy only in multiples of one unit. No source of red light can emit 1.5 units of energy, and therefore energy is said to be quantized. But is space also quantized? Can space be chopped into arbitrarily small size or is it also chunky like energy?

The earth revolves around the sun in a fixed orbit due to gravitational pull exerted by the sun on the earth but theoretically it can revolve in an orbit of any radius. (We are able to place a satellite around the earth in any orbit of our choice.) However, electromagnetic force unlike gravity is quantum in nature. Recall Bohr's model of hydrogen atom discussed in chapter five - the electron can revolve around the nucleus consisting of a proton only in orbits of fixed radii and each orbit has specific energy level. Now imagine that the proton and the electron both lose their electric charge, and as a result electromagnetic attraction between them ceases, leaving gravity the only force acting between them. Can the electron now revolve around the proton in any orbit or only in some fixed orbits? If the latter is the case, then gravity can be said to obey quantum laws. Gravity also allows singularity - the universe at the big bang could have been literally of zero size - but quantum theory prohibits it because the elementary particles cannot be confined in a region smaller than their wavelengths.

There is another way of looking at the difference between classical and quantum mechanics: Electromagnetic, strong nuclear and weak nuclear forces all operate through exchange of particles. For example, two charges repel or attract each other because they exchange photons, while gluons and W/Z particles are responsible for the strong nuclear force and the weak nuclear force respectively. But all attempts have failed to find a similar exchange particle, hypothetically called graviton, which mediates gravity.

The behaviour of gravity at microscopic scale will continue to be an enigma until a model is developed to reconcile quantum theory with gravity, without which what happened closer to the big bang will remain beyond our grasp. Every decade brings new hope of such a reconciliation, only to be belied later. There are a few competing hypotheses - we shall discuss them a little later - but none convincing enough to be accepted. However, if scientists do ultimately find a Theory of Everything (ToE) that unifies all the four fundamental forces in nature, how close will we be to unravelling the greatest of all mysteries - the origin of the cosmos? The ToE will be able to answer the how question of the origin but definitely not the why question. The hypothetical ToE is only a law which the universe follows but why this law and not any other will remain an open question. Are there many possible ToEs, each describing a different type of universe or is ours the only possible universe? At this point science reaches its limit and even a great scientist like Stephen Hawking yields to philosophy:

> Even if there is only one possible unified theory, it is just a set of rules and equations. What is it that breathes fire into the equations and makes a universe for them to describe? The usual approach of science of constructing a mathematical model cannot answer the questions of why there should be a universe for the model to describe. Why does the universe go to all the bother of existing? Is the unified theory so compelling that it brings about its own existence? Or does it need a creator, and, if so, does he have any other effect on the universe? And who created him?[1]

The future of the universe is no less uncertain. We expected its expansion to slow down due to gravitational attraction between the galaxies; instead we have found that the expansion is speeding up under the influence of mysterious dark energy, about which we know very little. (Some very recent studies indicate that the conclusion of accelerating expansion might have been based on insufficient data and in reality it is not speeding up.)[2] If the expansion of the universe were slowing down, it would attain a maximum size at some point in the future before beginning to collapse, and then it would gradually contract, ending up in a big crunch. It would then be possible to imagine the universe as an endless cycle of big bangs and big crunches. However, a universe with a definite beginning but without any end is difficult to imagine. Eternity is a long time. We can only speculate what might happen 1 trillion years from now on the basis of our current knowledge of the universe, but that might change later. Ironically, an accelerating expansion will destroy the evidence of expansion as all other galaxies will ultimately be receding from us at a speed greater than the speed of light, preventing the light emitted by them from reaching us. We would not know that there are other galaxies in the universe.

The origin and evolution of life on the earth is also beset by similar problems. We do not know how life originated on the earth and why it remained struck in the simplest form of bacteria and archaea before suddenly evolving into a much more complex form called eukaryotes. Why have new 'body types' not been invented after the Cambrian explosion? We have many snapshots of life on the earth in the form of fossil records since it first emerged 3.5 to 4 billion years ago, which confirm the fact of evolution, but certainly it cannot be claimed that the entire path of evolution has been mapped and all the factors that drove the evolution are exactly known.

The biggest obstacle, however, in unravelling the mystery of life, is that consciousness lives in splendid isolation, preventing the long grasp of reason from touching it. We have no idea what consciousness is and how a material object acquires the ability of being conscious. Is consciousness a property of matter? If yes, all matter should possess consciousness, which is not the case. If consciousness emerges from organising matter in a complex form like our brain, which has been the materialistic view at least since the time of Carvaka, then it must cease with death. But the question is, "why are we not able to recreate it from the same matter?" Why can't we resurrect a dead person? Why can't we create life from matter? We have not been able to create even an artificial cell, let alone human mind. Conversely, if it is altogether a different non-material entity, which is not destroyed at the time of death, as claimed by *Vedantic* philosophers, then how does it interact with matter? The "content of consciousness", to use Wigner's phrase, of an earthworm cannot be the same as that of a human being. Does it mean that consciousness has also evolved along with material body over time?

Is consciousness completely different from matter and energy? Is it the third pillar of reality? It just exists. There are questions and questions, but no answers. *Vedanta* has long held the view that the cosmos has a soul - *Brahman* - which is all pervasive and a part of it also resides in every sentient being. Our perception that we exist separately from the cosmos is merely an illusion. Lynn Margulis, an American evolutionary biologist, who proposed the endosymbiosis theory of origin of eukaryote cells, saw merit in ancient *Vedantic* view:

> In a sense then, the Vedic intuition that individual awareness is illusory and that each of us belongs to a single primal ground - *Brahman* - may be accurate: we share a common heritage, not only of chemistry but of consciousness, of the need to survive in a cosmos whose matter we share but which is itself indifferent to our living and self-concern.[3]

The approach of science is reductionist. Matter is made of molecules and molecules of atoms. For long the atom was thought to be the smallest unit of matter, but then the electron was discovered followed by protons and neutrons. Now we know that neutrons and protons are not indivisible, as was thought earlier, but consist of quarks. The size of a hydrogen atom is of the order of 10^{-10} metre, that is, one metre divided by 10 billion. 1,00,000 protons can fit into the size of a hydrogen atom. The quarks and electrons are ten times smaller than the protons. As per the standard model of particle physics, the entire universe consists of no more than 17 different elementary particles, the particles that cannot be subdivided any further. They are not only constituents of all matter and energy but also mediators of three of four fundamental forces.

However, there is no guarantee that these elementary particles are indeed indivisible. Scientists have proposed 'string hypothesis' that claims that the elementary particles consist of one-dimensional strings. Imagine a sitar string, which produces notes of different frequencies (Sa, Re, Ga, Ma, Pa, Dha, Ni) depending on where the string is pressed. The vibration of the hypothetical string in different modes supposedly produces different elementary particles. Every elementary particle corresponds to a particular frequency of vibration, which gives the particle its characteristics like, mass, charge, spin etc. The only difference is that while the sitar strings are tied to a frame, the particle strings exist independently. They are either open at both the ends or form circular loops. However, these strings are incredibly small, of the order of 10^{-34} metre, a billion billion times smaller than the quarks and electrons. The kind of energy that would be required to detect these strings is much beyond the reach of the most powerful particle accelerators built by us. But even if the string hypothesis is experimentally confirmed it will be hard to claim with absolute certainty that the strings are indeed the smallest constituents of everything in this universe.

String hypothesis also attempts to unite quantum mechanics with the general theory of relativity. It proposes that space itself - and by extension time because space-time is a combined entity in the general theory - is made up of strings. The rival hypothesis called 'loop quantum gravity' postulates that space is made up of atoms, not ordinary atoms that are to be found in everyday stuff around us, but a special type of atom, incredibly tiny like the strings. These atoms are linked to one another that create the fabric of space. In either case, space no longer remains smooth and continuous. It becomes chunky and discrete like matter and energy. We are not able to observe the discreteness of space in our daily life because the quanta of space are very very small.

Reductionism faces another barrier. As the particle becomes smaller and smaller, it becomes more and more like a wave - a different type of wave called probability wave. Therefore, the particle does not exist at a point; rather it can be found anywhere in a region represented by a waveform. Of course, the probability of finding the particle at one point will vary from the probability at any other point. However, when the particle is actually observed, it is found at a particular point. Obviously, the very act of observing leads to the collapse of the probability waveform and the particle assumes a position when it encounters a conscious observer. At this point inadequacy of scientific reductionism is exposed as matter cannot be understood by further dividing it. Matter manifests only when it encounters the consciousness of an observer, a property of the 'whole', which cannot be divided in parts. The whole becomes more than the sum of its parts.

There was a great excitement during the times of Newton and Laplace that predicting the future accurately lay within the grasp of humanity. Laplace's assertion that subsequent state of any system can be predicted if we know its initial state and the forces acting upon it was the marker of that confidence. It was, however, soon realized that a large scale system becomes so chaotic that a very tiny change in the initial conditions can lead to a vastly different outcome. The last nail in the coffin of determinism was driven by quantum mechanics. Particles behave randomly at the microscopic level, making it impossible to predict the behaviour of an individual particle. They act as if they have consciousness of their own.

Therefore, the complete truth continues to frustrate us in many different and unexpected ways, as if somebody quietly shifts the goalpost the moment it comes within our striking distance. The truth in its completeness can never be known because of its very nature – every answer raises a few more questions. So what has been the result of centuries of human effort? There are two ways of looking at this: In one view, we are very close to the final answer. We may never be able to know the big bang itself but we know what happened, say, a nanosecond after that. We are creeping towards the final answer though more and more effort is producing less and less results. In any case, whatever remains unknown will not fundamentally alter our notion of the universe. Perhaps there is a limit to precision with which we can explore the truth and Godel's incompleteness theorem comes into play – a system cannot know everything about itself. We cannot know the complete truth because we are part of it.

The other view is that how much we do not know is unknown. We may have reached very close to the big bang, but new findings could radically change our understanding of the universe. We cannot really be sure about the significance of something that we do not know. Also, remember that we scarcely have any idea of dark matter and dark energy, which constitute most of the universe. Similarly, although we know the general contours of evolution, the specific details are still missing. And these arguments can be extended to any branch of knowledge. Which of the two views is correct? Again, we do not know. But what we can say with certainty is that discovering truth has been a fascinating journey for mankind, and it will continue to be so despite knowing that we may not ever reach the final destination.

And this journey has given us deep insight into the meaning of life. If two words could capture the essence of existence, they are 'paradox' and 'balance'. Life is paradoxical: If you acquire too much money, you have no time to enjoy it; if you have too much time at your hands, you do not have money to enjoy; if you have a one room house, five people live there; if you have a ten bedroom house, there are hardly two or three. There was hardly any instance of suicide in Nazi concentration camps but South Korea, which is a rich country, has very high suicide rate. Strange, that when death is imminent, you fight hard to escape it and want to live, and when life seems full of possibilities, you are inclined to end it. Such paradoxes are everywhere in life - economy, politics, society, and indeed nature. The second most important learning is that you have to strike a fine balance in every aspect of life in order to enjoy it with fullness. Life's journey is like treading on a razor's edge. Why is life paradoxical? Is it so because it contains multiple opposing tendencies within itself? Is balance required to build a bridge between the opposites? I leave these questions for the readers to ponder over.

Notes and References

1. *The Illustrated A Brief History of Time* by Stephen Hawking, pp 232-3, Bantam Books, New York, 1996.
2. Marginal Evidence for Cosmic Acceleration from Type Ia Supernovae, JT Nielsen, A Guffanti, and S Sarkar, Scientific Reports 6, No 35596; doi: 10.1038/srep35596 (2016).
3. *What is Life?* by Lynn Margulis and Dorion Sagan, p 48, University of California Press, Berkeley, 2000.

Bibliography

Anderson, Douglas P, *et al*, "Evolution of an Ancient Protein Function involved in Organized Multicellularity in Animals", *eLife* 2016; 5:e10147.

Ansari, SM Razaullah, Aryabhata I, "His Life and His Contributions", *Bulletin of the Astronomical Society of India*, Vol 5, 1977.

Aristotle, *The Nicomachean Ethics*, translated by DP Chase, George Routledge & Sons, 1910.

________, *On the Heavens*, translated by W.K.C. Guthrie, Harvard University Press, London, 1939.

Arons, AB and Peppard, MB, "Einstein's Proposal of the Photon Concept - A Translation of the Annalen der Physik Paper of 1905", *American Journal of Physics*, Vol 33, No 5, May 1965.

Aryabhata, *The Aryabhatiya of Aryabhata: An Ancient Indian Work on Mathematics and Astronomy*, translated by Walter Eugene Clark, The University of Chicago Press, 1930.

________, *Surya-Siddhanta*, translated by Rev Ebenezer Burgess, edited by Phanindralal Gangooly, University of Calcutta Press, 1935.

Baaaquie, Belal E and Willeboordse, Frederick H, *Exploring the Invisible Universe: From Black Holes to Superstrings*, World Scientific, Singapore, 2015.

Baker, Gregory L and Blackburn, James A, *The Pendulum: A Case Study in Physics*, Oxford University Press, 2005.

Bangs, C, Johnson Les and Matloff, Gregory, *Paradise Regained: The Regreening of Earth*, Copernicus Books, New York, 2010.

Bartusiak, Marcia (Eds), *Archives of the Universe: 100 Discoveries that Transformed Our Understanding of the Cosmos*, Vintage Books, New York, 2006.

Basham, AL, *The Wonder that was India*, Rupa & Co, New Delhi, 1989.

Beiser, Arthur, *Concepts of Modern Physics*, Tata McGraw Hill Education, Sixth edition, New Delhi, 2008.

Bentham, Jeremy, *A Fragment on Government*, Oxford Press, 1891.

________, *An Introduction to the Principles of Morals and Legislation*, Oxford Press, 1823.

Bhattacharya, Ramkrishna, *Studies on the Carvaka Lokayata*, Anthem Press, London, 2011.

Blair, Ann, "Tycho Brahe's Critique of Copernicus and the Copernican System", *Journal of the History of Ideas*, Vol 51, No 3, 1990.

Bodhi, Bhikkhu (Eds), *In the Buddha's Words: An Anthology of Discourses from the Pali Canon*, Wisdom Publications, Inc, Somerville, 2005.

Bodhitaru and Chinmaya, Prem (Eds), *Secrets of Yoga by Osho*, Penguin Books, India, 2004.

Born, Irene (Trans), *The Born-Einstein Letters: Correspondence between Albert Einstein and Max and Hedwig Born from 1916 to 1955*, The McMillan Press Ltd, London, 1971.

Born, Max, *The Statistical Interpretation of Quantum Mechanics in Nobel Lectures in Physics* (*1942-1962*), World Scientific, Singapore, 1998.

Bowler, Peter J, Charles Darwin: *The Man and His Influence*, Cambridge University Press, 1996.

Brickman, PD and Campbell, DT, "Hedonic Relativism and Planning the Good Society" in *Adaptation Level Theory: A Symposium*, edited by Appley, MH, Academic Press, New York, 1972.

Brickman, PD, Coates, D and Janoff-Bulman, R, "Lottery Winners and Accident Victims: Is Happiness Relative?", *Journal of Personality and Social Psychology*, Vol 36, No 8, 1978.

Brownlee, Donald and Ward, Peter D, *Rare Earth: Why Complex Life is Uncommon in the Universe*, Copernicus Books, New York, 2003.

Burchfield, Joe D, "Darwin and the Dilemma of Geological Time", *Isis*, Vol 65, No 3, 1974.

Campbell, Lewis and Garnett, William, *The Life of James Clerk Maxwell: With a Selection from His Correspondence and Occasional Writings and a Sketch of His Contributions to Science*, Cambridge University Press, 2010.

Carpi, Anthony and Egger, Anne E, *The Process of Science*, Visionlearning, New Canaan, USA, 2011.

Chaichian, Masud, Rojas, Hugo Perez and Tureanu, Anca, *Basic Concepts in Physics: From the Cosmos to Quarks*, Springer-Verlag, Heidelberg, 2014.

Copernicus, Nicholas, *On the Revolutions*, Vol 2, edited by Jerzy Dobrzycki, translation and commentary by Edward Rosen, The Macmillan Press Ltd, London, 1978.

Cordon, Luis A, *Freud's World: An Encyclopedia of His Life and Times*, Greenwood, Santa Barbara, California, 2012.

Csikszentmihalyi, Mihaly, *Flow and the Foundations of Positive Psychology: The Collected Works of Mihaly Csikszentmihalyi*, Springer Netherlands, 2014.

Curtis, Heber and Shapely, Harlow, "The Scale of the Universe", *Bulletin of the National Research Council*, Vol 2, Part 3, No 11, May 1921.

Darwin, Charles, *The Origin of Species*, PF Collier & Son, New York, 1909.

________, *The Variation of Animals and Plants under Domestication*, Volume II, John Murray, London, 1868.

Davisson, CJ, "The Diffraction of Electrons by a Crystal of Nickel", *Bell System Technical Journal*, Vol 7, No 1, 1928.

Dawkins, Richard, *The Greatest Show on Earth: The Evidence for Evolution*, Free Press, New York, 2009.

Dreyer, John Louis Emil, *Tycho Brahe: A Picture of Scientific Life and Work in the Sixteenth Century*, Cambridge University Press, 2014.

Durkheim, Emile, *Suicide: A Study in Sociology*, translated by John A Spaulding and George Simpson, The Free Press, New York, 1997.

Dusheck, Jennie and Tobin, Allan J, *Asking about Life*, Third edition, Brooks/Cole, Belmont, USA, 2005.

Duve, Christian de, *Life Evolving: Molecules, Mind, and Meaning*, Oxford University Press, New York, 2002.

Easterlin, Richard, "A Puzzle for Adaptive Theory", *Journal of Economic Behaviour and Organization*, Vol 56, No 4, 2004.

________, "Does Economic Growth Improve the Human Lot? Some Empirical Evidence", in *Nations and Households in Economic Growth: Essays in Honor of Moses Abramovitz*, edited by David, Paul and Reder, Melvin, Academic Press, Inc, New York, 1974.

Eddington, Arthur, *The Mathematical Theory of Relativity*, Cambridge University Press, 1960.

Faraday, Michael, "Experimental Researches in Electricity", *Philosophical Transactions of the Royal Society of London*, Vol 122, No 122, 1832.

Finocchiaro, Maurice A (Ed and Trans), *The Essential Galileo*, Hackett Publishing Company, Inc, Indianapolis, 2008.

Freund, Ida, *The Study of Chemical Composition: An Account of its Method and Historical Development*, Cambridge University Press, 2014.

Galilei, Galileo, *Dialogue Concerning Two New Sciences*, translated by Henry Crew and Alfonso de Salvio, Cosimo Classics, New York, 2010.

Gandhi, Mahatma, *The Bhagavad Gita: According to Gandhi*, Orient Publishing, New Delhi, 2016.

Geiger, H, "On the Scattering of the α-Particles by Matter", *Proceedings of the Royal Society of London A*, Vol 81, No 546, 1908.

Geiger, Hans and Marsden, Ernest, "On a Diffuse Reflection of the α-Particles", *Proceedings of the Royal Society of London A*, Vol 82, No 557, 1909.

Geison, Gerald L, *The Private Science of Louis Pasteur*, Princeton University Press, New Jersey, 1995.

Gilbert, William, *De Magnete*, translated by P Fleury Mottelay, Dover Publications, Inc, New York, 1958.

Gingerich, Owen, *God's Planet*, Harvard University Press, Cambridge, 2014.

________, "Truth in Science: Proof, Persuasion, and the Galileo Affair", *Perspectives on Science and Christian Faith*, Vol 55, No 2, 2003.

Greene, Brian, *The Elegant Universe: Superstrings, Hidden Dimensions, and the Quest for the Ultimate Theory*, Vintage, London, 2000.

Grey, Aubrey de and Rae, Michael, *Ending Aging: The Rejuvenation Breakthroughs That Could Reverse Human Aging in Our Lifetime*, St Martin's Griffin, New York, 2007.

Guffanti, A, Nielsen, JT and Sarkar, S, "Marginal Evidence for Cosmic Acceleration from Type Ia Supernovae", *Scientific Reports* 6, No 35596; doi: 10.1038/srep35596 (2016).

Hagerty, Michael R and Veenhoven, Ruut, "Wealth and Happiness Revisited: Growing National Income Does Go with Greater Happiness", *Social Indicators Research*, Vol 64, No 1, 2003.

Hanh, Thich Nhat, *The Heart of the Buddha's Teaching: Transforming Suffering into Peace, Joy, and Liberation*, Harmony Books, New York, 2015.

Hawking, Stephen, *The Illustrated A Brief History of Time*, Bantam Books, New York, 1996.

Henig, Robin, *The Monk in the Garden: The Lost and Found Genius of Gregor Mendel, the Father of Genetics*, Mariner Books, New York, 2001.

Hooke, Robert, *Micrographia or Some Physiological Descriptions of Minute Bodies*, Cosimo Classics, New York, 2007.

Hubble, Edwin, "A relation between distance and radial velocity among extra-galactic nebulae", *PNAS*, Vol 15, No 3, 1929. http://www.freakonomics.com/2011/06/21/the-suicide-paradox-full-transcript (accessed on 22 October 2017)

James, Michael, *Happiness and the Art of Being: An Introduction to the Philosophy and Practice of the Spiritual Teachings of Bhagvan Sri Ramana*, Fourth PDF edition, CreateSpace, 2012

Jenkin, Fleeming, "Review of 'The Origin of Species'", *The North British Review*, Vol 46, No 92, 1867.

Jha, Dr Ganganatha, *The Chandogyopanishad*, Poona Oriental Book Agency, 1942.

Johnson, George, *Miss Leavitt's Stars: The Untold Story of the Woman Who Discovered How to Measure the Universe*, Atlas Books, New York, 2005.

Kahneman, Daniel, *Thinking, Fast and Slow*, Farrar, Straus and Giroux, New York, 2013.

Kahneman, Daniel, Katz, Joel and Redelmeier, Donald A, "Memories of Colonoscopy: A Randomized Trial", *PAIN*, Vol 104, No 1, 2003.

Kennedy, Robert F, "Robert F Kennedy Speeches". https://www.jfklibrary.org/Research/Research-Aids/Ready-Reference/RFK-Speeches/Remarks-of-Robert-F-Kennedy-at-the-University-of-Kansas-March-18-1968.aspx (accessed on 22 October 2017)

Kiehl, Jeffrey, "Lessons from Earth's Past", *Science*, Vol 331, No 6014, 2011.

Koonin, Eugene V, *The Logic of Chance: The Nature and Origin of Biological Evolution*, Pearson Education, Inc, USA, 2011.

Kragh, Helge, *Niels Bohr and the Quantum Atom*, Oxford University Press, 2012.

Krishnananda, Swami, Commentary on the Bhagavadgita, The Divine Life Society, Rishikesh, India. https://www.swami-krishnananda.org/bgita/Commentary_Bhagavadgita.pdf (accessed on 26 October 2017)

________, *The Chhandogya Upanishad*, The Divine Life Society, India, 2004.

________, *The Mandukya Upanishad*, The Divine Life Society, Rishikesh, India.
https://www.swami-krishnananda.org/mand/Mandukya_Upanishad.pdf (accessed on 26 October 2017)

________, *The Philosophy of the Panchdasi*, eBook, The Divine Life Society, India.
https://www.swami-krishnananda.org/panch/Philosophy_Panchadasi.pdf (accessed on 6 November 2017)

Lane, Nick, *The Vital Question: Why is Life the Way It Is*, Profile Books, 2016, London.

Lee, Ronald, "The Demographic Transition: Three Centuries of Fundamental Change", *Journal of Economic Perspectives*, Vol 17, No 4, 2003.

Leewenhoeck, Anthony, "An Abstract of a Letter from Mr Anthony Leewenhoeck", *Philosophical Transactions of the Royal Society of London*, Vol 14, No 159, 1684.

Lester, David, "Suicide and Culture", *World Cultural Psychiatry Research Review*, Vol 3, No 2, 2008.

Livingston, Dorothy, *The Master of Light: A Biography of Albert A Michelson*, The University of Chicago Press, Chicago, 1979.

Lyons, Timothy W, Planavsky, Noah J and Reinhard, Christopher T, "The Rise of Oxygen in Earth's Early Ocean and Atmosphere", *Nature*, Vol 506, No 7488, 2014.

Magner, Lois N, *A History of the Life Sciences*, Third edition, Marcel Dekker, Inc, New York, 2002.

Malhotra, Rajiv, *Indra's Net: Defending Hinduism's Philosophical Unity*, HarperCollins Publishers India, 2016.

Mancosu, Paolo, "Acoustics and Optics" in *The Cambridge History of Science*, Volume 3, *Early Modern Science*, edited by Roy Porter, Katharine Park and Lorraine Daston, Cambridge University Press, 2006.

Margulis, Lynn and Sagan, Dorion, *What is Life?*, University of California Press, Berkeley, 2000.

Matteucci F, Sozzetti A and Spitoni, E, "The Galactic Habitable Zone of the Milky Way and M31 from Chemical Evolution Models with Gas Radial Flows", *Monthly Notices of the Royal Astronomical Society*, Vol 440, No 3, 2014.

Maxwell, James Clerk, "A Dynamical Theory of the Electromagnetic Field", *Philosophical Transactions of the Royal Society of London*, Vol 155, 1865.

Mehra, Jagdish (Ed), *The Collected Works of Eugene P Wigner*, Part B, Volume 6, Springer-Verlag, Berlin, 1995.

Morrison, John C, *Modern Physics: for Scientists and Engineers*, Academic Press, USA, 2009.

Myers, David G, *The Pursuit of Happiness: Discovering the Pathway to Fulfilment, Well-Being, and Enduring Personal Joy*, HarperCollins, New York, 1992.

Neumayer, Eric, "Are Socio-economic Factors Valid Determinants of Suicide? Controlling for National Cultures of Suicide with Fixed-Effects Estimation", *Cross-Cultural Research*, Vol 37, No 3, 2003.

Newman, Stuart A and Niklas, Karl J, *Muticellularity: Origins and Evolution*, Preface, xxi, The MIT Press, Cambridge, 2016.

Newton, Sir Isaac, *Four Letters from Sir Isaac Newton to Doctor Bentley Containing Some Arguments in Proof of a Deity*, London, printed for R&J Dodsley, Pall-Mall, 1756.

________, *Mathematical Principles of Natural Philosophy and His System of the World*, Vol 2, Motte's translation revised by Florian Cajori, University of California Press, Los Angeles, 1934.

________, *Mathematical Principles of Natural Philosophy*, translated by Andrew Motte, First American edition, Daniel Adee, New York, 1848.

O'Flaherty, Wendy Doniger, Dreams, *Illusion and other Realities*, The University of Chicago Press, Chicago, 1986.

Oersted, HC, "Experiments on the Effect of a Current of Electricity on the Magnetic Needle", *Annals of Philosophy*, Vol 16, No 94, 1820.

Osho, *Absolute Tao: Subtle is the Way to Love, Happiness and Truth*, Osho International, Mumbai, 2012.

Paz, Octavio, "In Search of the Present: Nobel lecture". https://www.nobelprize.org/nobel_prizes/literature/laureates/1990/paz-lecture.html (accessed on 22 October 2017)

________, *The Labyrinth of Solitude*, Grove Press, Inc, New York, 1985.

Pedersen, Olaf, *A Survey of the Almagest: With Annotation and New Commentary by Alexander Jones*, Springer, New York, 2010.

Penrose, Roger, *The Emperor's New Mind: Concerning Computers, Minds and the Laws of Physics*, Vintage, London, 1990.

Pierre-Simon, Marquis de Laplace, *A Philosophical Essay on Probabilities*, translated by FW Truscott and FL Emory, Cosimo Classics, New York, 2007.

Plopper, George, *Principles of Cell Biology*, Second edition, Jones & Bartlett Learning, USA, 2016.

Poincare, Henri, *Science and Method*, translated by Francis Maitland, Dover Publications, Inc, New York, 2003.

Prabhupada, A.C. Bhaktivedanta Swami, Bhagavad Gita As it is, Bhaktivedanta Book Trust International, Inc., USA, 1989.

Prasad, Ramananda, "Free Will, Karma, Reincarnation, Effort, and Grace". http://www.gita-society.com/bhagavad-gita-section4/4_Free will.htm (accessed on 21 October 2017)

Rajneesh, Bhagwan Shree, *The Way of Tao: Discourses on Lao Tse's Tao-Te-King*, Part II, translated by Dolli Didi, Motilal Banarsidass, Delhi, 1979.

Ramasubramanian, K, Srinivas, MD and Sriram, MS, "Modification of the Earlier Indian Planetary Theory by the Kerala Astronomers (c 1500 AD) and the Implied Heliocentric Picture of Planetary Motion", *Current Science*, Vol 66, No 10, 1994.

Rees, Martin, *Just Six Numbers: The Deep Forces that Shape the Universe*, Basic Books, New York, 2000.

Regis, Edward, *What is Life?: Investigating the Nature of Life in the Age of Synthetic Biology*, OUP, New York 2009.

Relethford, John H, *Human Population Genetics*, Wiley-Blackwell, New Jersey, 2012.

Rossing, Thomas D (Ed), *Springer Handbook of Acoustics*, second edition, Springer-Verlag, Berlin, 2015.

Rutherford, Ernest, "Bakerian Lecture: Nuclear Constitution of Atoms", *Proceedings of the Royal Society of London A*, Vol 97, No 686, 1920.

———, "The Scattering of α and β Particles by Matter and the Structure of the Atom", *Philosophical Magazine*, Vol 21, No 125, 1911.

Sagan, Carl, *Cosmos*, Ballantine Books, New York, 1980.

Schrodinger, Erwin, *What is Life?: With Mind and Matter and Autobiographical Sketches*, Cambridge University Press, 2012.

Schwann, Theodor, *Microscopical Researches into the Accordance in the Structure and Growth of Animals and Plants*, The Sydenham Society, London, 1847.

Sen, Amartya, *Development as Freedom,* Oxford University Press, 2001.

________, *On Ethics and Economics,* Oxford University Press, New Delhi, 1990.

________, *The Economics of Life and Death,* Scientific American, May 1993.

________, *et al, The Standard of Living, The Tanner Lectures,* edited by Geoffrey Hawthorn, Cambridge University Press, 1988.

Shastry, Vyas, "How Aryabhata Got the Earth's Circumference Right?". https://www.livemint.com/Sundayapp/8wRiLexg1N2IOXjeK2BKcL/How-Aryabhata-got-the-earths-circumference-right-millenia-a.html (accessed on 15 August 2018)

Szanton, Andrew, *The Recollections of Eugene P. Wigner: As Told to Andrew Szanton,* Springer, 1992.

Thomson, JJ, "Cathode Rays", *Philosophical Magazine and Journal of Science,* Vol 44, No 269, 1897.

Tiner, John Hudson, *Exploring the World of Astronomy: From Center of the Sun to Edge of the Universe,* Master Books, USA, 2013.

Tucker, Tom, *Bolt of Fate: Benjamin Franklin and His Electric Kite Hoax,* Public Affairs, New York, 2003.

Voelkel, James R, *Johannes Kepler and the New Astronomy,* Oxford University Press, New York, 1999.

Volta, Alessandro, "On the Electricity Excited by the Mere Contact of Conducting Substances of Different Kinds", *Philosophical Magazine,* London, Vol 7, No 28, 1800.

Weinberg, Steven, *The First Three Minutes: A Modern View of the Origin of the Universe,* Basic Books, New York, 1993.

Wellman, HM and Woolley, JD, "Children's Conceptions of Dreams", *Cognitive Development,* Vol 7, No 3, 1992.

Whittaker, ET, A History of the Theories of Aether and Electricity, Dover Publications, Inc., New York, 1951.

Wilkinson, Will, In Pursuit of Happiness Research: Is It Reliable? What Does It Imply for Policy?, Policy Analysis No 590, April 11, 2007, Cato Institute.
https://www.cato.org/publications/policy-analysis/pursuit-happiness-research-is-it-reliable-what-does-it-imply-policy (accessed on 4 November 2017)

Wynn-Williams, Gareth, *Surveying the Skies: How Astronomers Map the Universe,* Springer International Publishing, Switzerland, 2016.

Young, Thomas, "The Bakerian Lecture: Experiments and Calculations relative to Physical Optics", *Philosophical Transactions of the Royal Society of London*, Vol 94, 1804.

Zee, A, "An Old Man's Toy" in *E=Einstein: His Life, His Thought, and His Influence on Our Culture*, edited by Donald Goldsmith and Marcia Bartusiak, Sterling, New York, 2006.

Index